ETIQUETTE

OF

GOOD SOCIETY

EDITED AND REVISED BY

LADY COLIN CAMPBELL

"There is no outward sign of good manners but has a deep foundation in morals."—GOETHE

CASSELL AND COMPANY LIMITED
LONDON PARIS & MELBOURNE
1893
All rights reserved

PREFACE.

It may be said that the books already published on the subject of "manners" and "etiquette" are sufficiently numerous for the wants of the community; but to this remark we would reply, that although the broad principles of manners remain the same, yet the *minutiæ* are continually altering and varying, and modes of speech and action which were considered the height of politeness a few years ago would be pronounced, at any rate very *old-fashioned* if used and exhibited in the present day. As this is shown to be the case more fully in the Introduction, it is only necessary to state here for what purpose the subjects treated have been chosen, and why they have been placed in the order in which they will be found.

Christenings, Weddings, and Funerals seem to be the subjects which stand most prominently forward in the catalogue of social observances, hallowed as they are by sacred rites and ceremonies; attached to and consequent on these principal events are a host of minor circumstances, which also demand attention.

Birth—the commencement of life—with all its attendant ceremonies, is naturally the first subject considered. The next three or four chapters are devoted to a description of all the conventional forms and arrangements necessary to be known by the neophyte on his or her entrance into society. Etiquette, Letter-Writing, Visiting, the Toilet—a thorough knowledge of all these subjects will save the timid maiden and the shy youth from awkward embarrassment when obliged to act on their own responsibility.

Then Marriage is considered, and consequent on that all the onerous duties it entails on the married couple in their new position in life, as Host and Hostess; the various ways in which they may show hospitality to their friends in connection with the table, by the giving of Breakfasts, Luncheons, Dinners, Teas, and Suppers, which may be great or small, grand or simple, according to the wishes and means of the donors themselves.

The different amusements, in-door and open-air, which may be provided for the entertainment of their guests are next described, such as the arrangements necessary for Dances, Picnics, Private Theatricals, Garden Parties, and sports of various kinds.

Presentation at Court, the subject of the nineteenth chapter, is an episode in the life of comparatively few people, it is true; but still it demands a place in this volume. The closing scene of life, and the last sad offices performed by the survivors, naturally form the subject of the final chapter.

CONTENTS

CHAPTER I.
INTRODUCTION.

                                                                PAGE.

The Existence of a Code of Manners in Early Times—Manners of the Last Century—Necessity of Good Manners—On Polish—"A Gentleman"—"A Lady"—Titles of Honour—Heraldry ... ... 9—24

CHAPTER II.
BIRTH.

Old Customs - Private Baptism—Public Baptism—Godparents—Christening Presents—The Christening—Confirmation—Age required—Preparation—Dress necessary—The Ceremony ... ... 25—34

CHAPTER III.
ETIQUETTE AND SOCIAL OBSERVANCES.

Origin of the Word "Etiquette"—The Distinguishing Mark of Good Manners—Against Extreme Ceremony, Excessive Apologising, and Affectation—The Laws of Introduction—Attentions to be paid by a Gentleman to a Lady—Different Modes of Bowing and Shaking the Hand—The Walk—The Carriage—Conversation—Voice—Laughter—Inaccuracies of Speech—Laws of Precedency ... ... 35—52

CHAPTER IV.
LETTER-WRITING.

How to Write a Letter—"Pens, Ink, and Paper; Sealing-wax and Wafer"—Different Forms of Invitation — Modes of Addressing Persons of Rank ... ... 53—61

CHAPTER V.
VISITING.

The Use of "Calling"—Occasions when Calls should be paid—The Card-case and its Contents—Ceremonies of Calls—Cake and Wine—Visits—Length of Visits—Conduct when Staying in a Friend's House—Gratuities to Servants ... ... 62—74

CHAPTER VI.
THE TOILET.

Neatness—Suitability—Style of Dress appropriate for Christenings—When paying Calls—At Garden Parties—Picnics—The Seaside—Lawn Tennis—Morning Dress—Dinner and Ball Dresses—Jewellery—Bride's Costume; Bridesmaids'—Guests at a Wedding—Mourning—Man's Dress—As a Bridegroom—At Garden Parties—"Full Dress"—Jewellery—Hat and Gloves ... ... 75—89

CHAPTER VII.
MARRIAGE.

"Things to be thought of"—Interview with Father-in-Law—Engagement Ring—Wedding Presents—Etiquette of Courtship—The Bridesmaids—The Licence and Banns—Bridegroom's Presents to Bride and her Maids—Day before the Wedding—Wedding Day—Ceremony—Breakfast—Departure ... 90–106

CHAPTER VIII.
HOUSEHOLD APPOINTMENTS.

Variety of Household Appointments—A good Manager—Styles proper for different Rooms—Breakfast, Dining, and Drawing Rooms—"Best Rooms"—Temperature of Rooms—Laying the Table—List of Requisites for entertaining Twelve People 107—114

CHAPTER IX.
BREAKFASTS.

Eating and Drinking—Breakfasts in Particular—Break-

CONTENTS. vii

PAGE

fasts in the Olden Time—In the Present Day—How to Set the Table, and what to put on it—Wedding Breakfasts—Hunt and Sportsmen's Breakfasts—Breakfast Dishes for the different Seasons ... 115—123

CHAPTER X.
LUNCHEONS.

Manners at Table—What to place there, and how to place it—Hot Luncheons—Cold Luncheons 124—127

CHAPTER XI.
DINNERS.

"The Dinner Question"—Dinner Tables of the last Ten Centuries—Good Cookery—Waiters—Invitations—Whom to Invite—Dinner *en Famille* and *à la Russe*—Carving—Table Appointments and Decorations—Arrival of Guests—The Dinner—Wines—Dessert—Retirement of the Ladies—Coffee—Tea—Departure ... ... 128—154

CHAPTER XII.
TEAS.

High Teas—What to put on the Table—Arrangement of Drawing-room—Afternoon Teas ... ... 155—159

CHAPTER XIII.
SUPPERS.

Appointments of the Table—French Display—Our Supper Tables—Impromptu Suppers—Hot Suppers ... ... 160—164

CHAPTER XIV.
BALLS.

Public Balls—How to Manage them—Tickets—Introductions—Duties of Stewards—Fancy Dress Balls—Private Balls—Rooms necessary—Music—Lights—Decorations—Cloak Rooms—Tea, Drawing, and Ball Rooms—Card Room—Duties of the Entertainers to their Guests—Of Partners to their Partners—"Cinderella Dances" ... . 165—176

CONTENTS.

CHAPTER XV.
PRIVATE THEATRICALS.

Charades—Tableaux Vivants—Wax-work Exhibitions
—Private Theatricals 177–185

CHAPTER XVI.
GARDEN PARTIES.

Lawn Tennis Parties 186–189

CHAPTER XVII.
EXCURSIONS AND PICNICS.

Private Picnics—Conveyance of Guests and Provisions
—Subscription Picnic—Election and Duties of a
Manager—Provisions and Beverages ... 190–194

CHAPTER XVIII.
FIELD SPORTS AND AMUSEMENTS.

Hunting—Shooting—Fishing—Boating—Tricycling—
Skating 195–202

CHAPTER XIX.
THE COURT.

Buckingham Palace—Who may be Presented—Court
Dress — Rules and Regulations — The Drawing-
Room—The Levée — The Irish Court — Court
Mourning 203–209

CHAPTER XX.
DEATH.

Things to be done immediately upon a Death—Old
Customs—The Funeral—The Mourners—The Service—Reading of the Will—Inquiries by Friends—
Acknowledgments—Sunday after the Funeral—
Monuments 210–216

THE

ETIQUETTE OF GOOD SOCIETY

CHAPTER I.

INTRODUCTION.

The Existence of a Code of Manners in Early Times—Manners of the Last Century—Necessity of Good Manners—On Polish—"A Gentleman"—"A Lady"—Titles of Honour—Heraldry.

> "A man by nothing is so well bewrayed
> As by his manners, in which plaine is shewne
> Of what degree and what race he is growne."
> *"Faërie Queene."*

FROM very early times a Decalogue—if we may be allowed to use the term—of Manners has existed. In the "ancient bokes" of the Anglo-Saxons we find directions given to our ancestors what to do and what not to do. Their Norman successors, too, though not distinguished for the politeness which is said to characterise their descendants, had their code of manners set forth; and so down to the present day, through every successive age, the necessity for, and the importance of, an established form has been invariably recognised. But as the ideal of what constitutes true politeness is continually changing, or rather, let us say, the modes of showing politeness are continually changing—for the principle remains the same at all times and in all places—so there constantly arises a necessity for the revision of old rules and for setting forth the accepted code of manners for the present time.

The gentlefolk of a few centuries back would prove rough guests at a modern dinner-table, however carefully they observed the rules laid down. "Never set on fyshe, flesche, ne fowle, more than two fyngers and a thombe." Our forefathers are also cautioned not to pick their teeth with "knife, strawe, nor stick"; nor to clean them on the table-cloth. To wipe the mouth on the table-cloth was allowable, but not the nose or eyes! In the reign of Stephen it was considered etiquette to cough very loud when entering a house, "for there may be something doing which you ought not to see." A guest at table is recommended "to keep his nails clean, for fear the fellow next him should be disgusted." There are many unmentionable habits spoken of as common which we should regard with unmitigated horror, but which the people of that day looked upon as ordinary and correct behaviour. Happily for us, time and civilisation have swept away all these rough-and-ready usages; and it may be safely said that a man will now find his superiors more accessible, his equals more at their ease, and his inferiors more mannerly, than in the most golden age of the olden time.

Even since the last century, manners have altered strangely. The great freedom then permitted, both in words and action, is no longer allowed. We need scarcely mention the well-known fact that ordinary conversations were richly besprinkled with oaths by the "good old English gentlemen," and gentlewomen too, if what is related of a certain Duchess of Marlborough be true. The story goes that she went to call upon Lord Mansfield on business, and, not finding him within, declined to leave her name. His lordship's secretary, in describing the unknown, said: "I could not make out, sir, who she was; but she swore so dreadfully that she must be a lady of quality!" And we read in Dr. Johnson's life—"This evening one of our married ladies, a lively, pretty little woman, *good-humouredly* sat down upon Dr. Johnson's knee, and, being encouraged by the company, put her hands round his neck and kissed him." As no note of exclamation follows the record of this incident, we are led to the conclusion that it was not regarded as extraordinary or unbecoming.

It was at as late a period as the last century, too, that the following violent fun was thought admissible:—A large strong table-cloth was spread on the upper steps of the staircase, and upon this cloth the ladies seated themselves in rows; then the gentlemen took hold of the lower end, attempting to pull it downstairs. The ladies resisted with all their might. The contest invariably ended by the cloth and the ladies being pulled down to the bottom of the stairs, "when," says the relater, "everything was found bruised but modesty."

Then, if we turn from our own people and look at other nations, we find that they too have had their lessons to learn, and have learnt them.

The Russian nobleman of to-day, with his polished, gentlemanly bearing and his studied politeness to superiors and inferiors alike, forms a strong contrast to his forefathers, who are said to have "dropped both pearls and vermin as they walked along!" and whom the great Catherine found it necessary to prohibit striking their wives in public; while the wives were forbidden to wash out their mouths in the drinking glasses.

In France also, the home and centre of politeness and good-breeding, judging from the experiences of an English traveller, manners were not at one time equally refined. "At Madame Du Bocage's, a lady of high rank, the footman took the sugar in his fingers and threw it into my coffee. I was going to put it aside; but hearing that it was made on purpose for me, I e'en tasted Thomas's fingers. The same lady would needs make tea *à l'anglaise.* The spout of the teapot did not pour freely; she bade the footman blow into it!" We may exclaim, with Hannah More, "Are these the beings who are called polite?"

Enough has been said to show the wide difference which exists between ancient and modern manners and customs. In the following chapters we shall consider more minutely the present code of social laws which should regulate our external conduct and behaviour.

For the present we may affirm that the maxim "Manners makyth man" has the same force as ever. Goodness of heart, however boundless; learning, however profound; and accomplishments the most brilliant and varied, are not in themselves sufficient to make us pleasant and agreeable members of society—a knowledge and practice of the laws of good-breeding must be added to make a perfect whole. Your character may be inestimable; but if you speak loudly, or with a vulgar twang, if you are boisterous in your behaviour, and eschew *les convenances* of society, your best friends will—behind your back—lament that you are so little endowed with manners, although "an excellent creature." "Manners recommend, prepare, and draw people together; in all the clubs manners make the members; manners make the fortune of the ambitious youth—for the most part, his manners marry him, and he marries manners." The principal and groundwork of these laws is, that they tend to add materially to the happiness and comfort of those around us, smooth and soften the contact of the individual atoms which are incessantly coming against each other in the restless intercourse of the busy world, and add a charm to the quiet monotony of everyday life. Amid the multitude of thorns which encompass this daily life, every flower that will grow should be cultivated with care. Acts of attention and thoughtfulness shown to those around not only make their days pass more easily and happily, but at the same time ennoble the doer, and provoke a sweet return of kindly feeling and good-will. Lord Chesterfield, who, says Hannah More, "adorned conversation by his wit as much as he impaired it by his principles," has defined "politeness to be the art of pleasing." St. Paul, "one of the few writers with whom this accomplished peer was *not* acquainted," remarks this censorious lady, recommends, with as much warmth as his lordship, the duty of pleasing his neighbour; but here the two moralists part company. "The noble writer would have us please others to benefit ourselves; the Christian writer directs us to please others for their good. The essence of the worldly code of ethics is selfishness, that of the Christian is disinterestedness."

It is the opinion of a French writer* that "la vraie philosophie respecte les formes autant que l'orgueil les dédaigne : il faut une discipline pour la conduite comme il faut un ordre pour les idées" (True philosophy respects forms as much as pride despises them : we require a discipline for our conduct, just as we require an order for our ideas).

It is said by foreigners, in speaking generally of the English, that we as a nation lack what is called polish; but they assign to us the character of solidity. Now, hard, solid bodies are those that take the highest polish. The material, then, is fine, hard, and close, delicate and good; and English men and women, if they so will it, may shine like mirrors to the rest of the world. Only let them be careful not to mistake varnish for polish. It is only soft bodies, which admit of little polish, that require the former, and it is applied to hide all flaws and to conceal the meanness of the material beneath its surface. But, however thickly it may be laid on, the false covering will chip here and there, and the gloss will only be superficial, and will never, in reality, equal that of true polish of the grain.

Gentlemen and ladies—how much those words are abused! what various twisted and deformed ideas are connected in different persons' minds with those words! What more common expression among the vulgar than "He's quite the gentleman," "She is a real lady," and yet what various meanings are attached to them? Sometimes high birth is denoted; sometimes perfect manners; sometimes merely wealth; the fact of living an idle life, or profuse

---

* Portalis.

liberality. This last is the idea of the poor, who almost invariably measure a man or woman by the tightness or looseness of their purse-strings, and term them gentleman or lady accordingly. Originally a gentleman was defined to be one who, "without any title of nobility, wears a coat-of-arms, or whose ancestors have been freedmen." By-and-by two other classes crept into the circle. A man could be a gentleman by office and in reputation as well as those who were born such. According to Blackstone—"Whosoever studieth the laws of the realm, who studieth in the universities, who professeth the liberal sciences, and who can live idly and without manual labour, and well bear the port, charge, and countenance of a gentleman, he shall be called master and taken for a gentleman." But in the present day these three distinctions of birth, education, or wealth *alone* do not entitle their possessors to bear the "grand old name of gentleman." Something else must be added to make the perfect whole. "To have pride of gentrie is right gret folie, for oft time the gentrie of the bodie bemireth the gentrie of the soule; and we ben al of o fader and of o moder," says Chaucer.

"The *rank* is but the guinea *stamp*,
The man's the gowd for a' that,"

sings the Scottish bard in those often-quoted lines; and there is much fine gold without the stamp, no doubt. Yet we by no means wish to underrate the value of gentle birth and blood. Race tells in man as in any other animal, but it must not be considered as the only thing requisite. A man cannot say, "I am well-born, and *therefore* I am a gentleman." Neither will education stand alone. The head may be well stored with learning, the whole of the sciences may be "professed," and all the laws of the realm studied, and still a man may not have that within him which is essential to the claim of being a gentleman.

Wealth—ay, even the wealth of the Indies—is also futile in itself. Riches compass many things, but not this. A man may possess broad acres, and be surrounded with all the luxuries that money can command, and yet may be clothed in vulgarity, and steeped in vice from top to toe. Shall we designate such a one as "a gentleman"? What are the qualities, then, necessary to give a claim to this title? This is Chaucer's test—

> " Whoso is vertuous,
> And in his path not outrageous.
> When such one thou seest thee beforne
> Though he be not gentil borne,
> Thou mayst well sein (this is in sothe)
> That he is gentil because he dothe
> As longeth to a gentil man."

The different classes of the order of gentlemen are thus quaintly described by another old writer. He divides them under the heads of "Gentle gentle," "Gentle ungentle," and "Ungentle gentle":—"The gentle gentle are those of noble birth, who join to their gentle house gentle manners and noble conditions, which is the cause of the other word called gentle. Gentle ungentle is that man which is descended of noble parentage, by the which he is commonly called gentle, and hath in him such corrupt ungentle manners as to the judgment of all men he justly deserveth the name of ungentle. Ungentle gentle is he which is born of a low degree, which man, taking his beginning of a poor kindred, by his virtue, wit, policy, industry, knowledge of laws, and such like honest means, becometh a well-behaved and high-esteemed man." Thackeray defines a gentleman to be one "who is honest, gentle, generous, brave, and wise; who possesses all these qualities and exercises them in the most graceful outward manner."

Qualities such as these are not the mere accident of birth, nor the invariable accompaniments of wealth. None of them necessarily endow a man with delicacy of feeling, kindness of heart, courteousness of manner to his fellow-man—be he peer or peasant—chivalrousness to all women, in short, that fineness of nature so admirably delineated by Ruskin. "A gentleman's first characteristic," he says, "is that fineness of structure in the body which renders it capable of the most delicate sensation, and of that structure of the mind which renders it capable of the most delicate sympathies, or, as one may simply say, fineness of nature.

"This is, of course, compatible with heroic bodily strength and mental firmness; in fact, heroic bodily strength is not conceivable without such delicacy. Elephantine strength may drive its way through a forest and feel no touch of its boughs, but the white skin of Homer's Atrides would have felt a bent rose-leaf, yet subdue its feelings in the glow of battle, and behave itself like iron. I do not mean," continues the writer, "to call the elephant a vulgar animal; but if you think about him carefully, you will find that his non-vulgarity consists in such gentleness as is possible to elephantine nature; not in his insensitive hide, nor in his clumsy foot, but in the way he will lift his foot if a child lies in his way, and in his sensitive trunk, and his still more sensitive mind and capability of pique in points of honour. Hence it will follow that one of the probable signs of high breeding in men generally will be their kindness and mercifulness—these always indicate more or less firmness of make in the mind."

But we must e'en turn our attention to the "lady"—who has been for so long a time kept waiting, while the opposite sex were criticised and scrutinised—and see how the true gentlewoman may be distinguished from the counterfeit. If it be true, as the French say, that—

> " Les hommes font les lois,
> Les femmes font les mœurs," *

it is, indeed, highly necessary to decide what qualities are necessary to make "a perfect woman."

Women in their course of action describe a smaller circle than men, but "the perfection of a circle consists not in its dimensions, but in its correctness," says the logical Hannah More.

A true lady will be quite natural and easy in her manners, and this will have the effect of putting those at their ease who are in her company, whatever their station in life may be. She will shrink from all affectation and avoid all pretension, and never try, by any means, to appear other than she really is. She will be courteous to all around her, modest but not awkwardly bashful; brave, without being in the slightest degree bold or masculine; deferential and reverential to the aged, cheerful and lenient to the young; in fact, she will not only try

* De Ségur.

"to make *men* happy and to keep them so," but every living creature around her.

A quiet dignity will pervade all her actions. She is one who—

> "Hath a natural wise sincerity,
> A simple truthfulness, and these have lent her
> A dignity as moveless as the centre."

Her good manners will be in daily use, and not donned and doffed with company dress, and more especially a lady will never attempt to patronise in the slightest degree.

A high-bred gentlewoman will never be proud and haughty in her demeanour to others, but there are those "who with haughty steps would walk the globe o'er the necks of humbler ones."

We once saw a so-called lady at a London fête asked by another lady, who was on the point of fainting from the heat, to pass a glass of water. The fashionably dressed and splendidly jewelled woman regarded the suppliant with a haughty and indignant stare, for presuming to ask her to perform a menial act, and immediately moved away.

It is a very mistaken notion, and yet one held by many, although perhaps not confessed, that a lady demeans herself by manual labour, and that if she wishes to keep her title to the name, she must lead an aimless, useless, idle life. Now our ways and habits have been so gradually altered by civilisation that ladies do lead very different lives from their ancestresses. Here is the account of the manner in which Elizabeth Woodville, born in a very high station, and afterwards wife of King Edward IV., was accustomed to spend an ordinary day :—" Rose at four o'clock, and helped Catherine to milk the cows. Six o'clock, breakfasted ; the buttock of beef too much boiled, and the beer a little of the stalest. Seven, went to walk with the lady my mother in the courtyard. Ten, went to dinner. Eleven, rose from table, the company all desirous of walking in the fields. Four, went to prayers. Six, fed the hogs and poultry. Seven, supper on the table. Nine o'clock, the company fast asleep—these late hours are very disagreeable."

English ladies of the nineteenth century are not expected to milk cows and feed pigs, but if circumstances obliged them to do these or any other similar acts of labour, what we would impress on our readers' minds is that they would not necessarily cease to be "ladies" in the proper sense of the word. "She openeth her mouth with wisdom, and in her tongue is the law of kindness. She looketh well to the ways of her household, and eateth not the bread of idleness. Her children arise up and call her blessed, her husband also, and he praiseth her."

We may here mention, *en passant*, the "titles of honour" borne by certain classes of gentlefolk, and the different degrees of rank which exist. Titles of honour are designations which certain persons are entitled to claim as their right, in consequence of certain dignities being inherent to them. They vary according to the rank of their possessor. The titles of Emperor, King, and Prince denominate the highest rank; then come the orders of the nobility, which are five in number, namely—Duke, Marquis, Earl, Viscount, and Baron. All these dignities are hereditary, and the wives and children of peers have likewise their appropriate titles of honour. Another dignity which brings with it the right to a title of honour is a Baronetcy—and this, too, is hereditary. Below the Baronet comes the Knight, but Knighthood is not hereditary; it expires with the life of the possessor, and does not descend to the heir as do all the other titles. In this last category may be placed ecclesiastical dignities— academical, legal, and municipal distinctions—which have their several titles of honour pertaining to their offices, but like that of knighthood do not descend. Mention must also be made of the title of Esquire, although the general use of it by those who are not strictly speaking entitled to it has virtually destroyed it as a distinctive dignity. Those to whom it *legally* belongs are—the eldest sons of Knights, and the eldest sons of younger sons of the nobility, by virtue of birth. Justices of the Peace, Officers of the Queen's Court and Household, and of Her Majesty's Navy and Army, by virtue of office. Doctors of Law, Barristers, and Physicians are reputed Esquires; but at the present time this line of demarcation is growing every day more faint, and the title of Esq. is used as a mere "title of courtesy" given to every gentleman of presumed respectability, and though it may be occasionally abused, there can be no doubt that it is on the whole exceedingly convenient. The various and proper forms for addressing persons of different degrees of rank will be given in a following chapter.

We are now brought to the subject of Heraldry. Heraldry has been stigmatised as "a science of fools with long memories"; it should rather be designated as a study which, properly directed, would make fools wise. Heraldry is the art of arranging and explaining in proper terms all that appertains to the bearing of coats-of-arms or badges, and other hereditary or assumed marks of honour.

The twelfth century is the earliest period to which can be traced the bearing of heraldic devices properly so called, and they became hereditary about the commencement of the following century.

Heraldry owes its origin to the Crusades. During these memorable wars, the principal leaders of the different armies found it necessary to be distinguished by some outward sign, so that amidst the confusion and tumult of battle a friend could be detected from a foe, in spite of the close-fitting disguise of armour worn by all alike. And so a device was placed upon the shield which at that time was always carried to battle. The various distinctive coats-of-arms—birthrights of our nobility, of which there are five orders—are displayed on shields, escutcheons, or banners. There is another sign of gentle birth, the crest. This is next to the shield in point of antiquity. It was originally the ornament worn upon the helmet in the far-off days of which we have been speaking. Lastly, there are mottoes. These trace their origin to those same days of chivalry, and were the war-cries of the different knights.

When a man marries he impales his wife's paternal arms by placing them upright on the left side of his own in the same escutcheon. If his wife be an heiress the husband may bear her arms on an escutcheon over his own. The children retain only the father's coat-of-arms, unless they inherit property from their mother likewise.

A story is related of a lady who wished to die before her husband, because if he died first she could not put his coat-of-arms on his tomb, he being not a man of family; "but," said she, "if I die first he can claim a right of placing my arms on my tomb, because I am a woman of quality by birth."

The arms of a widow are composed of her husband's and her father's impaled within a lozenge. Those of a maiden lady are her father's only, borne in a lozenge also. Ladies are not allowed the use of crests.

If the husband be a Knight of the Garter or of any other order, the arms of the wife must not be impaled, but placed in a separate shield.

Heraldic devices have been called the hall-marks of the nobility, but in the present day these ancient prerogatives have been usurped and appropriated by ignorant yet aspiring people, and sold over and over again by unscrupulous traders who minister to the bad taste of would-be gentlefolk.

It is a cause for great regret that such a noble science as that of heraldry should be allowed to be open to the mercy of charlatans, who arrange and blazon coats-of-arms at complete variance with personal history and in violation of all precedent.

It is considered a misdemeanour, and punished as such, to infringe on a merchant's mark, and yet the marks of our nobility are purloined continually by those who only bear the name of the family and cannot trace the faintest line of their descent.

"Crests is my leading article, but I do deal in 'scutcheons," once said a "professor" of heraldry who kept a "studio." "They come for cheap crests as advertised; but when I once get them in my *mediveal* office, under the influence of a dim religious light through stained glass—to sit in my antique chairs and behold my *libary*, presided over by an old suit of armour—it is all 'up' with them, and they take anything." Crests are the portions most affected, but shields and mottoes are daily appropriated.

There are shops where a busy trade goes on in sales of this description. You state your name, and have no need for any anxiety on the subject. A crest is sure to be discovered. If your name happens to be a noble one, you have all the more for your money. "Russell, did you say, sir? a very noble crest—goat *passant*. Sketch, ten shillings and sixpence; with *casque* and mantling in proper colours, one guinea and a half; illuminated in vellum, two guineas," and so on; proving the assertion that in this brazen age anything can be got with money.

CHAPTER II.

BIRTH.

"Old Customs"—Private Baptism—Public Baptism—Godparents—Christening Presents—The Christening—Confirmation—Age Required—Preparation—Dress Necessary—The Ceremony.

> "It might have been seven o'clock in the evening when Mr. Kenwigs sent out for a pair of the cheapest white kid gloves—those at one shilling and twopence per pair—and, selecting the strongest, walked down-stairs with an air of pomp and much excitement, and proceeded to muffle the knob of the street-door knocker therein."—"*Nicholas Nickleby.*"

THE ceremony performed by Mr. Kenwigs would greatly excite the curiosity of passers-by nowadays, and any proud father who ventured to imitate him would be regarded as an exceedingly eccentric gentleman, if nothing more; but at one time it was considered quite the "correct thing" to clothe the knocker in white kid on the birth of a child, and the little Kenwigs was by no means the only infant whose advent was announced in this manner. Of course the original purpose was to deaden the noise made by impatient postmen and other callers. Thus it answered two purposes. At Haarlem and some other Dutch towns the arrival of a little Hollander is proclaimed by means of a small placard which is adorned with red silk and lace; this is affixed to the door of the house, and when the friends and neighbours, being thus apprised, call to pay their respects to the mother and inspect the new-comer, they are regaled with mulled wine and cinnamon cakes.

Formerly in this country the friends who, directly the news reached them, called to offer their congratulations were entertained on these occasions with caudle, which is a kind of spiced gruel flavoured with rum. The cups out of which this refreshment was partaken were made for and used only on these special occasions. They were of china and had two handles, one on either side, so that the gossips could easily pass them on from one to the other "when so dispoged."

Caudle cups were often handed down as heirlooms, and as such were highly prized by our ancestresses, who made much more stir and "to-do" on these occasions than is now the custom. Then there was the "gentlemen's party"—this took place at a later date. At the end of a fortnight, if mother and child were doing well, it was the custom for the husband to entertain *his* particular friends. Both bachelors and Benedicts were invited to eat "sugared toast," which, as the cookery books say, was thus prepared:—

"Rounds of bread toasted, and each stratum spread thick with moist sugar; these were piled up in a portly punch bowl. Strong beer was in the meantime heated, and poured boiling hot over the mound of bread."

This "Gothic mess" was taken immediately to the expectant guests and quickly demolished. At the conclusion of the repast each visitor put a piece of money into the empty bowl, and the contents were presented to the—for the time being—ruler of the household, the "nurse." Often, too, good strong ale was brewed, or a pipe of wine laid by, to be drunk on the majority of the child.

Times are changed, old customs and ceremonies have in great measure gradually died out, and no new ones seem to have arisen in place of them. An event of this kind calls forth very few ceremonies nowadays; yet these must be observed in due order and according to the fashion of the time.

Some doctors expect the fee on these occasions immediately after the birth; others make a stated charge for attendance during the illness and receive their fee when they cease to attend at the house.

Friends and acquaintances either call and leave or send their cards by their servants, with kind inquiries, but the mother and child are not disturbed in their seclusion until the former acknowledges the kindness and courtesy of her friends, and announces her reappearance in society by sending her card in return. It is usual to fix for the christening to take place, if possible, as soon as the mother is well enough to go out, when her infant is about a month old.

In days gone by, this rite was performed when the child was but three days old. King Edward VI. and his sisters were baptised at that early age, and the ceremony—which lasted between two and three hours—took place at night by torch-light. The child was carried under a canopy, preceded by gentlemen bearing in state the sponsors' gifts, and attended by flourish of trumpets.

Altogether the royal christenings of those days must have been most fatiguing and venturesome proceedings—at any rate, to the mother; for though she did not accompany her child to the chapel, she was removed on to a state pallet, where she received congratulations, and whence the procession started. That it was the general custom for the baptism to take place very soon after the birth may be gathered from Mr. Pepys, who writes in his voluminous Diary—" We went to Mrs. Brown's, where Sir W. Pen and I were godfathers, and Mrs. Jordan and Slopman were godmothers. And there, before and after the christening, we were with the woman above in her chamber. I did give the midwife ten shillings, and the nurse five shillings, and the maid two shillings. But, inasmuch as I expected to give the name to the child, but did not, I forbore then to give my plate which I had in my pocket, namely, six spoons and a porringer of silver."

If an infant is feeble when born, and not expected to live, the rite of baptism is at once performed privately in the room in which the child is. In cases of extreme necessity, where the assistance of a clergyman cannot be procured, any person may baptise the child. Lay baptism is an irregularity, not a nullity. Should a child die before being baptised, it may be interred in consecrated ground, but the burial service of the Church cannot legally be read over its grave.

If the child lives, it is subsequently " received " into the Church, and then receives its sponsors. Baptism should be performed in the parish in which the child is born. The selection of godparents is often a matter of considerable delicacy and difficulty; for many people are reluctant to accept the office, while others again, who think they have a strong claim to the honour, are offended if they are overlooked.

Formerly there were two godfathers and two godmothers. Now, if the infant be a boy, he has two godfathers and one godmother; and if a girl, then the order is reversed. The godparents are chosen from the relatives and friends of the parents. For the first-born the sponsors should be near relatives, preference being given to the father's family. It is not advisable to choose elderly people for this office; for, although its duties are supposed to cease with confirmation, yet the association often lasts a lifetime, and kindly help and counsel may be given in later days by the godparent to the godchild, should the battle of life prove hard, should parents die, or friends depart. At a baptism which took place in 1744, the sponsors must have been very aged relatives, judging from their kinship to the infant. Its godmothers were three in number—its great-great-grandmother, great-grandmother, and great-great-great-aunt. Its great-great-great-great-uncle and two of its great-great-uncles were the godfathers.

There is not much variety in the choice of the christening presents. The old-fashioned gift of "knife, fork, and spoon" has given place to what is more useful—a silver basin and spoon, which in babyhood holds bread and milk, and afterwards serves as a sugar bowl. But the silver mug and handsomely-bound Bible still hold their ground. A set of coral beads was formerly a common gift, more especially to a "baby-girl." Coral was deemed to possess certain valuable properties most beneficial to children; not only was it good to rub their gums with, but it also had the power of preserving them from the "falling sickness"; for we are assured that the best coral "worn about the neck will turn pale and wan if the child who wears it be sick, and comes to its former colour again as its wearer recovers health."

We lately heard of a godfather, evidently of a practical turn of mind, who, considering the ordinary kind of presents more ornamental than useful, bought for his little godson some shares in a mine to the amount that he would have spent on him in a silversmith's shop. It is not usual to consult the sponsors as to the choice of the name; but when the parents are desirous to pay a special compliment to one or other of the godparents, they give their child the same name as that borne by the sponsor.

The christening ceremony, as appointed by the Church of England (of which we are now speaking), sometimes takes place during divine service, but generally speaking is performed by itself and in the morning.

The day being fixed, all interested assemble at the church appointed. The officiating clergyman, followed by the sponsors and the nurse and child, proceeds to the font. As at a wedding, it is now customary for only those who have some office assigned them to form the principal group. The father and mother, and any other friends who may be present, take their seats in pews near to the font.

The child is held by the godmother during the first part of the service, and she places it on the left arm of the clergyman when he is ready to receive it. When he says the words, "Name this child," the chief godfather should pronounce it audibly and distinctly. The nurse, who should stand on the clergyman's right hand—the godmother on his left—takes the child from him, and the service proceeds to its conclusion.

The father accompanies the clergyman to the vestry after the service, in order to give particulars necessary for registration, and also to distribute the proper fees.

Legally, none can be claimed for a baptism, but custom has established the practice. The amount bestowed depends very much upon the ideas of the donor. Sometimes the clergyman receives a banknote, sometimes one or two guineas, according to the means and position of the parents. In London these ceremonials are most expensive—so many persons appear on the scene, all of whom expect gratuities. The beadle and the sexton, the woman who sweeps inside the church and the man who sweeps outside, the pew-opener and the clerk, are all ready with itching palms.

The rite of churching generally takes place immediately before that of the christening. The clergyman is requested to be at the church a short time before the hour appointed for the christening; and the churching service, which is but a short one, takes place before the sponsors arrive.

It will be seen that here, as well as in other chapters, the ceremonial of the Church of England has been taken for an example and alone described. It need hardly be remarked that the baptismal service is performed by other religious denominations according to other rites; but as it would be impossible in a book of this description to attempt to describe the many different forms, one only has been cited, as in every case, though the religious ceremonials differ, the social usages are similar.

The entertainments given on the christening day are various. Sometimes, when it takes place in a morning, the guests return to luncheon; sometimes they separate at the church door, and meet again in the evening at a dinner party given in honour of the young stranger. Whatever the festivity, the officiating clergyman is always invited, and the baby is exhibited either before or after the repast in all the splendour of its christening robe. The presents are often given at this time; sometimes they are sent afterwards. During the dinner the infant's health is proposed; and at dessert a christening cake, which closely resembles a wedding cake, appears, bearing a flag on which is emblazoned the name of the hero of the day. A small portion is often put safely away, to be eaten in after years by the one whose nativity is thus celebrated. A piece of cake and bottle of wine are sent out to the servants, who fully expect to drink the little one's health.

The nurse, too, generally receives a present on these occasions—a piece of money is slipped into her hand; and then again, when she takes the child for the first time to the houses of the friends of its parents to exhibit it, it has been usual to give her a present of money. In some parts the child is offered a gift of salt and an egg for good luck; special care being taken that the young pilgrim makes its first visit to the house of a near relative or particular friend, so that the ceremony will not be omitted or forgotten; for superstition says that if the ceremony be neglected, the infant will be exposed during life to the miseries of want.

Confirmation is, as it were, the sequel to baptism. The age at which bishops accept candidates for this rite is from fourteen to fifteen years.

Notices of confirmation to be held are always given out in the different churches some weeks prior to the event, and persons desirous of being admitted to the rite are requested to make known their wish, and to give in their names to their respective clergymen.

Classes are formed, and instruction and preparation given, during the weeks preceding the day which the bishop has appointed. At the hour named, the candidates, having previously received from their clergyman a card on which is written his or her name, and signed by their instructor, as a certificate that they have been prepared for the solemn service, proceed to the church in which the ceremony is to take place.

The young girls should be dressed in white. A high white dress, without shawl or jacket, and a white veil or cap, and white gloves, is the proper costume. If a veil is worn, it must be a simple square of white tulle falling equally over the front and back. Great simplicity should be observed in the dress for confirmation. The youths wear black suits, black ties and gloves. They are placed on one side of the church, and the maidens on the other.

When the time arrives for the laying-on of hands, the girls go first, either by two and two, or more, as may be the custom of the bishop. They give their card or certificate into the hands of the bishop's chaplain, who stands near to receive them. The candidates kneel down before the bishop, who lays his hand severally on their heads. When the short prayer repeated by him while doing so is finished, they rise from their knees and return to their seats. After all have been confirmed the bishop usually delivers a short address, which concludes the service.

CHAPTER III.

ETIQUETTE AND SOCIAL OBSERVANCES.

Origin of the word "Etiquette"—The Distinguishing Mark of Good Manners—Against Extreme Ceremony, Excessive Apologising, and Affectation—The Laws of Introduction—Attentions to be paid by Gentlemen to a Lady—The Different Modes of Bowing and Shaking the Hand—The Walk—Carriage—Conversation—Voice—Laughter—Inaccuracies of Speech—Laws of Precedency.

"I am the very pink of courtesy."
Shakespeare.

"Those graceful acts,
Those thousand decencies, that daily flow
From all her words and actions."
Milton.

CENTURIES ago the word "etiquette" conveyed to those who used it a far different signification than to us of the present day. The word—an Anglo-Norman one—originally specified the ticket tied to the necks of bags or affixed to bundles to denote their contents. A bag or bundle thus ticketed passed unchallenged.

Our ancestors, as we have seen, had their codes of manners. The chief rules of these forms of behaviour were written or printed upon cards or tickets, and thus the word "etiquette" gradually came to mean what we understand by it. Hence the modern slang phrase, "the ticket," is not so meaningless as it would seem to be.

Before beginning with the specialities of etiquette, let me remark that the first and great characteristic of what is called good-breeding is perfect ease of manner and the absence of all *fussiness*. Whatever the company we may be thrown into, whatever the circumstances, this quiet ease should never be allowed to forsake us, neither diverging into unbending stiffness on the one hand, nor into too much familiarity on the other. Perfect politeness requires presence of mind, a quick sense of propriety, and an ability to form an instantaneous judgment of what is fittest to be said and done on every occasion as it offers. "Il me semble que l'esprit de politesse est une certaine attention à faire que, par nos paroles et nos manières, les autres soient contents de nous et d'eux-mêmes" (I consider the spirit of politeness to be one which will govern our behaviour, so that by our words and actions others may be pleased with us and with themselves) is the opinion of Montesquieu. In our endeavours to be polite, we must be careful not to run into any extremes, but bear in mind that good manners show themselves where to the vulgar eye they are the least observable. Extreme ceremony is only the caricature of good-breeding; it produces contempt and embarrassment, not respect and ease.

As an instance of the absurdity of extreme punctilio, I may relate one which occurred in Spain. On the death of a certain queen of that nation, the officers of the crown and grandees of the kingdom assembled at the usual time to open her Majesty's will; but finding that the first lady of the queen's chamber, who ought by virtue of her office to have been present, was absent, the august body sent a messenger requesting her attendance. The first lady replied that it was her duty not to leave her deceased royal mistress, and that therefore the nobles must wait upon her. Thereupon ensued a negotiation which lasted no less than eight hours. As both sides remained inflexible, it was proposed that without rising from their seats or moving themselves, they should be *carried* to a room at an equal distance between their own apartment and that of the Lady High Chamberlain, who should be also carried to the same place, seated upon a high cushion in the same manner as she had sat in the queen's chamber, to the end that it might be said that neither side had made a step to meet each other. This ludicrous compromise was actually carried out.

If a person of higher rank desires you to step first into a carriage, it is better to bow and obey than to decline. Addison remarks, "A polite country squire shall make you as many bows in half an hour as would serve a courtier for a week"; "and there is," says the same writer, "infinitely more to-do about place and precedency in a meeting of justices' wives than in an assembly of duchesses."

Thus, we should not constantly repeat the name of anyone with whom we may be talking, nor should we make an excessive use of titles when conversing with people of rank. Tittlebat Titmouse exposed his ignorance of the habits of good society, not only by his flurried manner and great anxiety to show what the French call *des petits soins*, but also in his mode of talking with his noble host—"Oh, yes, my lord; quite so, your lordship; wouldn't have been behind time, your lordship, for a minute, my lord," &c. &c.

At the same time be it remembered that the other extreme must be guarded against—familiarity, too, "breeds contempt." It is only against the constant repetition of title or name that we utter a protest. Gentlemen and gentlewomen of the last century invariably addressed one another as Madam and Sir; the terms are now obsolete in ordinary conversation. An occasional interpolation of the name of the person with whom we are conversing is what is required, and more especially if we should happen to dissent in any degree, to contradict or to affirm.

For instance, "Do you think so?" "I believe I am right," would sound brusque if not rude; but attach the name, and see what a different effect, and how softened the sentences appear: "Do you think so, Lady Penrose?" "I believe I am right, Mr. Brown."

In speaking to a king or queen we address them as Your Majesty—other members of the Royal Family, as "Sir," or "Madam," and Your Royal Highness. A Duke or Duchess is addressed in ordinary conversation as "Duke" or "Duchess"; while a marquis or marchioness, or any of the nobility of lower rank, would be spoken to, without distinction of their special titles, as Lord So-and-So or Lady So-and-So.

Descending in the scale of titles, I would, in passing, remark that it is not etiquette to address those who possess such titles as Colonel, Captain, Doctor, &c., by such designations only, but to append their respective surnames, and also that nothing is more objectionable than to hear ladies speak of gentlemen by their surnames only, or juveniles address their parents as "Pa" and "Ma," after the fashion of the Misses Pecksniff. For "grown-up" children, the terms "Father" and "Mother" are more becoming than "Papa" or "Mamma." The pronoun "my" should be used in speaking of relatives generally, as "My father says so," "My uncle told me."

Apologising, again, is constantly carried to an ill-bred extreme. Numerous, profound, and reiterated apologies have the effect of making every one within hearing of them remarkably uncomfortable, and particularly the one who receives them. "Apologising," says a modern author,* "is a very desperate habit, and one that is rarely cured." As it is ill-mannered to express too much regret, so it is the essence of rudeness not to make any apology. Should you have the misfortune to injure either the person or the feelings of your neighbour, the formal "I beg your pardon" should be accompanied by an effort to prove the sincerity of the words, though it need not take the practical form given it by the poor Tittlebat Titmouse before alluded to, who, when he broke a glass dish, turned first to his host and then to his hostess with profuse apologies, and at the same time assured them that he would replace it with the best in London the very first thing in the morning.

Let me now say a few words upon affectation, by which I mean the adoption of peculiarities of

* O. W. Holmes.

speech, action, and demeanour which are not natural. "La moindre affectation est un vice," says Voltaire. Oddities and singularities may attend genius, but when they do so they are its misfortunes and its blemishes. For instance, while we admire the wisdom of Dr. Johnson, we cannot hold up his manners as an example to be followed. Here is a description—"In the intervals of articulation he made various sounds with his mouth, sometimes as if ruminating, or what is called chewing the cud, sometimes giving a half-whistle, or making his tongue play backwards from the roof of his mouth, as if clucking like a hen; and when exhausted by much talking he would blow out his breath like a whale." Now, although this gross behaviour could never become the fashion, yet other practices are adopted which have quite as little grace and elegance about them, and, not being natural to the individual who assumes them, destroy that ease of manner which it is so essential to attain. It is curious to notice that a description written in the seventeenth century of the various forms of affectation then in vogue is singularly applicable to the present day. "At one time it was fashionable to be short-sighted; a man would not own an acquaintance until he had first examined him through a (an eye) glass. The age no sooner recovered its sight than the blind were succeeded by the lame." Is not this a picture of some of the present follies of fashion? Have we not men with eye-glasses through which they cannot see, and women with affected limp, almost amounting to an awkward hobble, disfigurations most lamentable to those who are ridiculous enough to follow this absurdity of fashion?

And now let me speak of the various fixed forms of observance which should be our guide on those occasions where set forms are found to be necessary in order to avoid embarrassment and confusion. It will be well first to give the general rules, and mention the exceptions when the circumstances which would occasion a divergence are treated of hereafter. To begin with introduction: when a lady and gentleman are to be introduced to each other, the lady's permission should first be asked and obtained, and the office can only be performed by a common friend. Always introduce the gentleman to the lady, and never the lady to the gentleman. When the sexes are the same, present the inferior to the superior.

The etiquette observed is to accompany the gentleman to the lady, who, if seated, does not rise, and say, "May I," or "Allow me to introduce Mr. Sinclair—Miss Grant, Mr. Sinclair." Whereupon both bow, but do not shake hands, the introducer then retires, and the introduced at once enter into conversation. It is always the part of the lady to make the first intimation of recognition at their next meeting. A gentleman must not either bow or shake hands with a lady until she has made the first movement; neither must he, under any circumstances, fail to return her courtesies. If he meet her in the street, and sees she wishes to speak, he will immediately turn and walk in the direction in which she is going; if on horseback, he will dismount and lead his horse, and walk by her side, for on no occasion is it permissible for a lady to stand for any time while talking in a street. In the days of our Dutch king, it was customary for a gentleman when walking beside a lady to carry his hat in his hand or under his arm. The practice of walking arm-in-arm appears to be quite of comparatively modern date, but is now entirely abandoned, except on such occasions as going in to dinner, supper, etc. The custom of a husband and wife appearing arm-in-arm when their names are announced at a reception is altogether out of date. The lady enters first, and her lord follows after. In the same way couples do not walk arm-in-arm in the streets, unless to traverse some crowd. When two or more persons walked together, it was formerly the custom to hold each other by the hands. In the twelfth and thirteenth centuries it seems to have been the height of gentility to hold the lady by the finger only. If by any mischance a lady is in a crowd, the gentleman should precede her, in order to clear a path for her, and try to shield her as much as he possibly can from rude encounters; for on such-like gatherings honest John Bull thinks he does not show the true spirit of liberty unless he jostles, squeezes, and pushes his neighbours about as much as possible. A gentleman will follow a lady up and down stairs; he will get out of a carriage first, and offer his hand in order to assist her to alight; he will not use slang expressions when conversing with her; he will never smoke in the presence of a lady without first obtaining her permission, and if, when smoking out of doors, he meets any lady, be she friend or foe, he will take his cigar out of his mouth while passing her. "To be sure," says Dr. Johnson, " it *is* a shocking thing blowing smoke out of one's mouth into other people's mouths, eyes, and noses." The custom of withdrawing the glove before shaking hands with a lady is now a thing of the past. It originated in the knight taking off his iron gauntlet, which would have hurt the hand of his "faire ladye." No longer do we see gentlemen carrying a creased glove, or wearing one untidily large, in order to avoid the awkwardness of keeping the lady waiting while he drags it off. The well-fitting, tidy, comfortable one has taken its place, and may it long retain it!

As grace should attend all the movements, whether of man or woman, the manner of bowing, shaking the hand, walking, and speaking should be at once refined and elegant.

The bow should be a graceful bend, or inclination of the head; not a hasty movement, nor a stiff jerk. A gentleman should raise his hat, indeed, take it off his head, but not with a flourish, nor seize it with a sudden dash, as is now so often seen. There is great art in making a bow, dignified and stately, but at the same time neither stiff nor awkward; and how much more difficult is it than people suppose to shake hands well!

In what a variety of ways are our hands shaken in the course of the year, and how few of those ways are pleasant ones! Sometimes our hands are seized and violently agitated to and fro; at others, a limp, nerveless something is dropped into our outstretched palm, which shows no sign of life while in our possession. There are people who, from no feeling of affection, but simply from a vicious habit intended to express heartiness and cordiality, squeeze your fingers until the rings upon them enter into your flesh. Others—and I think this the most trying ordeal—retain your hand in theirs for a length of time, and ever and anon give it a little shake by way of adding *empressement* to their inquiries about your welfare. This latter custom is a very old-fashioned one, but now and again one is rendered uncomfortable by encountering it. No; each of these forms of hand-shaking is most irritating and objectionable. Take the hand offered you firmly; be careful to grasp the *hand*, not the fingers merely, which has a ridiculous effect; give it a gentle pressure, and then relinquish it; do not lift it up to shake, neither let it drop suddenly—heartiness and cordiality should be expressed, without the slightest approach to boisterousness.

I have often heard people say, "I can tell whether a man is a gentleman from his walk." I know that servants can be distinguished by the short abrupt steps they take; so, doubtless, a true lady can be discovered by her manner of walking. The following forms one of a code of manners drawn up by a Frenchman for the benefit of his countrywomen in the thirteenth century :—" Do not trot or run, and as you walk look straight before you with eyelid slow and fixed, looking forward to the ground at five toises (thirty feet) before you, not looking at or turning your eyes to man or woman who may be to your right or left, nor looking upwards, nor changing your look from one place to another, nor laughing, nor stopping to speak to anybody." It does not appear that this strict rule was for the special use of nuns or any religious body, but intended for the well-bred lady of the time.

But to return to " ye maiden of our own day": let her step be firm and her gait steady, let her not walk in too great a hurry, nor yet drag slowly along. Let her arms move with the natural motion of the body; they must neither swing to and fro nor dangle by the side.

> "Grace was in all her steps,
> In every gesture dignity."

A man's walk should differ from a woman's in that he should take a longer step, but steadiness of carriage and firmness of tread are as necessary in the one as in the other. Horace Walpole is described as always entering a room with knees bent and feet on tiptoe, as if afraid of a wet floor; but we are told that this affected style was quite *à la mode* in his day.

In the house a woman is allowed much less freedom of posture than a man; he may change his position in an infinity of ways, lounge and loll, cross his legs, do anything but sit on the edge of his chair or clasp his hands round his knee; but a woman must sit still. Addison thought that the one great end of a lady's learning to dance was that she might know how to sit still gracefully. The hands, if not occupied, are so apt to fidget either with each other, with some part of the dress, or face. Very often it is a nervous habit; but from whatever cause it may arise, it should be at once and finally repressed.

One more remark I must make before I close the chapter, and that is on conversation. "The tone of good conversation," says Rousseau, "is flowing and natural; it is neither heavy nor frivolous; it is lively without noise." The art of conversation consists as much in listening politely as in talking agreeably; therefore never interrupt anyone who may be speaking to you, and at the same time do not let your eyes wander to other objects, but keep them on the speaker, avoiding, however, the rude stare. We should never be demonstrative in our actions while speaking, nor should we either talk loudly or laugh boisterously; and the Persians say of noisy, unreasonable talk, "I hear the noise of the millstone, but I see no meal." Whispering is a great breach of good manners. It is young people, generally speaking, who commit this breach. Youth and high spirits, together with love of fun and frolic, make them forgetful or oblivious of the feelings of others, and they indulge in this reprehensible and rude habit—for rude it most undoubtedly is. Who has not seen a knot of young people cluster together in the corner of a room, and begin first to whisper and then to giggle? It may be that nothing was further from their thoughts or lips than to make remarks upon the company present; but such conduct always produces the impression on the minds of those outside the clique that they are the subject of those comments, and perhaps the objects of ridicule. Therefore, however strong the desire may be to have private fun and amusement, or to communicate secrets, it must not be given way to in public.

Happily for us, general society is not made as uncomfortable by this style of behaviour as it used to be; for the following description of the misery endured by a gentleman at an evening party, written fifty years ago, would be deemed a highly exaggerated one now:—

"On my arrival the ladies indeed rose; but when I was seated, they grouped themselves in a corner and entered into a private cabal, seemingly to discourse upon points of great secresy and importance, but equal merriment and diversion. Their conversation was confined wholly to themselves—it was a continued laugh and whisper; a whole sentence was scarce ever spoken aloud; single words now and then broke forth, such as 'odious,' 'horrible,' &c. My friend seemed to be in an uneasy situation at his own table, but I was far more miserable. I sat mute, and seldom dared to raise my eyes or turn my head, lest by some awkward gesture I might draw upon me a whisper or a laugh." I should not have remarked upon this habit had it been an obsolete one; but it is by no means uncommon now.

Would that the speaking voice were as assiduously cultivated as the singing voice, and then the nerves of our ears would not be so often jarred by harsh and unmelodious talking! "Her voice was ever soft, gentle, and low—an excellent thing in woman." That it is a question of culture we may be sure, by observing that all those who speak on the stage have sweetly-toned, pleasant voices, and this could not be natural in every case. Our two Queens Anne and Mary were both distinguished for their clear and distinct pronunciation, their sweetness of intonation and grace of enunciation; these important accomplishments they derived from the instructions of Mrs. Betterton, an actress.

And then again, what pleasanter sound than a musical laugh? and yet how seldom do we hear one! Goldsmith asserts that a loud laugh bespeaks a vacant mind, and Carlyle writes in his quaint way, "Few are able to laugh what can be called laughing, but only sniff and titter from the throat outwards, or, at best, produce some whiffling, husky cachinnations, as if they were laughing through wool. Of none such comes good." Without endorsing this sweeping assertion, we may earnestly recommend the culture of a well-modulated voice and musical laugh.

But, alas! what avails the sweetest-toned voice, if the language is not correct and refined? In the words of Ruskin, "A well-educated gentleman may not know many languages—may not be able to speak any but his own. But whatever languages he knows, he knows precisely; whatever word he pronounces, he pronounces rightly—above all, he is learned in the peerage of words; knows the words of true descent and ancient blood at a glance from words of modern canaille." Not only should the rules of grammar be attended to strictly, not only should the "poor letter H" be always put in its right and never in its wrong place, but care should be taken lest words and phrases should be introduced unconsciously into our conversation, which are offensive corruptions of the English tongue. And to quote Ruskin once more, "Vulgarity is indicated by coarseness of language, but only so far as this coarseness has been contracted under circumstances not necessarily producing it. There is no vulgarity in—

> 'Blythe was she but and ben,
> And weel she liked a Hawick gill,
> And leugh to see a tappit hen';

but much in Mrs. Gamp's inarticulate 'bottle on the chumley-piece, and let me put my lips to it when I am so dispoged.' Provincial dialect," he goes on to say, "is not vulgar, but Cockney dialect is so in a deep degree, because it is the corruption of a finer language continually heard." This ignorance or want of taste meets with a sharp rebuke in the pages of the *Tatler*. The fashion of abbreviating words, of making one word out of two, and pronouncing the first syllable only, in a word that has many, is strongly censured. This reproof was directed against the use of such words as "phiz," "coz," and the like, then in vogue. We may, in like manner, condemn as wholly objectionable the use of those barbarous mutilations of phrases such as "thank you," which has been condensed into "thanks;" and also lift up our voices against the shortening of "invitation" into "invite." The constant use of the word "lady" and the term "lady friend" is also objectionable. It is to be presumed that all your female acquaintances are "ladies." A writer sarcastically observes, "There is scarce one *woman* to be met with; the sex consists almost entirely of *ladies*."

The recognised order of precedency is as follows :—

Peers rank among themselves by date, according to their patent of creation.

Foreign ambassadors are given the precedence of our nobility, as the representatives of the person of the Sovereign who accredits them.

There is no specified place for physicians or medical men, but they are ranked in the Royal household as next to knights.

PRECEDENCY AMONG MEN.

Sovereign.	Brothers of Sovereign.
Prince of Wales.	Uncles of Sovereign.
Other Sons of Sovereign.	Sovereign's brothers' or sisters' sons.
Grandsons of Sovereign.	

Archbishop of Canterbury, Lord Primate of All England.
The Lord High Chancellor or Lord Keeper.
The Archbishop of York, Primate of England.
The Archbishop of Armagh, Primate of Ireland.
The Archbishop of Dublin.
The Lord High Treasurer.
The Lord President of the Privy Council.
The Lord Privy Seal.
The Lord Great Chamberlain.
The Lord High Constable.
The Earl Marshal.
The Lord High Admiral.
The Lord Steward of Her Majesty's Household.
The Lord Chamberlain of Her Majesty's Household.
Dukes, according to their patent of creation.
Marquises, according to their patent of creation.
Dukes' eldest sons.
Earls, according to their patents.
Marquises' eldest sons.
Dukes' younger sons.
Viscounts, according to their patents.
Earls' eldest sons.
Marquises' younger sons.
Bishops—London, Durham, and Winchester. All other English Bishops according to their seniority of consecration.
Bishops of Meath and Kildare. All other Irish Bishops according to their seniority of consecration.
Secretaries of State of the degree of Baron.
Barons, according to their patent.
Speaker of the House of Commons.
Commissioners of the Great Seal.
Treasurer of Her Majesty's Household.
Comptroller of Her Majesty's Household.
Master of the Horse.
Vice-Chamberlain of Her Majesty's Household.
Secretaries of State under the degree of Baron.
Viscounts' eldest sons.
Earls' younger sons.
Barons' eldest sons.
Knights of the Most Noble Order of the Garter.
Privy Councillors.
Chancellor of the Exchequer.
Chancellor of the Duchy of Lancaster.
Lord Chief Justice of the Queen's Bench.
Master of the Rolls.
Lord Chief Justice of the Common Pleas.
Lord Chief Baron of the Exchequer.
The Lords Justices of the Court of Appeal in Chancery.
Vice-Chancellors.
Judges and Barons of the degree of the Coif of the said Courts.
Commissioners of the Court of Bankruptcy.
Viscounts' younger sons.
Barons' younger sons.
Baronets of England, Scotland, and Ireland.
Knights of Grand Crosses of the Bath.
Knights of Grand Crosses of St. Michael and St. George.
Knights Commanders of the Bath.

ETIQUETTE AND SOCIAL OBSERVANCES. 51

Knights Commanders of St. Michael and St. George.
Knights Bachelors.
Companions of the Bath.
Cavaliers Companions of St. Michael and St. George.
Eldest sons of younger sons of peers.
Baronets' eldest sons.
Eldest sons of Knights of the Garter.
Eldest sons of Knights of the Bath.
Knights' eldest sons.
Younger sons of younger sons of Peers.
Baronets' younger sons.
Esquires of the Sovereign's Body.
Gentlemen of the Privy Chamber.
Esquires of Knights of the Bath.
Esquires by creation.
Esquires by office.
Younger sons of Knights of the Garter.
Younger sons of Knights of the Bath.
Younger sons of Knights Bachelors.
Clergymen, Barristers-at-law, Officers in the Navy and Army, who are all Gentlemen, and have their respective precedency in their several professions.
Citizens.
Burgesses.

PRECEDENCY AMONG WOMEN.

The Queen.
Princess of Wales.
Princesses, daughters of the Sovereign.
Princesses and Duchesses, wives of the Sovereign's sons.
Granddaughters of the Sovereign.
Wives of the Sovereign's grandsons.
The Sovereign's sisters.
Wives of the Sovereign's brothers.
The Sovereign's aunts.
Wives of the Sovereign's uncles.
Wives of eldest sons of Dukes of the Blood Royal.
Daughters of Dukes of the Blood Royal.
Duchesses.
Marchionesses.
Wives of the eldest sons of Dukes.
Daughters of Dukes.
Countesses.
Wives of eldest sons of Marquises.
Daughters of Marquises.
Wives of younger sons of Dukes.
Viscountesses.
Wives of eldest sons of Earls.
Daughters of Earls.
Wives of younger sons of Marquises.
Baronesses.
Wives of eldest sons of Viscounts.
Daughters of Viscounts.
Wives of younger sons of Earls.
Wives of eldest sons of Barons.
Daughters of Barons.
Maids of Honour.
Wives of younger sons of Viscounts.
Wives of younger sons of Barons.

Wives of Baronets.
Wives of Knights of the Garter.
Wives of Knights of Grand Crosses, Order of the Bath.
Wives of Knights Grand Crosses of St. Michael and St. George.
Wives of Knights Bachelors.
Wives of Companions of the Bath.
Wives of Companions of St. Michael and St. George.
Wives of the eldest sons of the younger sons of Peers.
Wives of eldest sons of Baronets.
Daughters of Baronets.
Wives of the eldest sons of Knights of the Garter.
Daughters of Knights of the Garter.
Wives of eldest sons of Knights of the Bath.
Daughters of Knights of the Bath.
Wives of eldest sons of Knights Bachelors.
Daughters of Knights Bachelors.
Wives of younger sons of younger sons of Peers.
Wives of younger sons of Baronets.
Wives of Esquires of the Sovereign's Body.
Wives of Esquires to the Knights of the Bath.
Wives of Gentlemen entitled to bear arms.
Daughters of Esquires entitled to bear arms who are Gentlewomen by birth.
Daughters of Gentlemen entitled to bear arms who are Gentlewomen by birth.
Wives of Clergymen, Barristers-at-law.
Wives of Officers in the Navy and Army.
Wives of Citizens.
Wives of Burgesses.

CHAPTER IV.

LETTER-WRITING

Letter-writing in General—How to Write a Letter—" Pens, Ink, and Paper, Sealing-wax and Wafer "—Different Forms of Invitation—Modes of addressing Persons of Rank.

> " To write aptly is of practice;
> —— to write is to speak beyond hearing,
> And none stand by to explain." *Tupper.*

IT is said that orators write affectedly, ministers obscurely, poets floridly, learned men pedantically, and soldiers tolerably when they can spell. "No talent among men hath more scholars and fewer masters." The palm of good letter-writing has been universally awarded to the fair sex, but now-a-days, when so much correspondence goes on daily, few letters are indited which are really worthy of commendation. The lives we lead are so crowded with events that we have not the time to record them except in the most concise form possible; continual change, hurry, and bustle prevent us devoting much time to our pens, even although we have every incentive to write. Our more industrious and persevering ancestors wrote under difficulties, with their parchment or paper placed on their knees; while we possess desks of the most approved shapes and sizes, and have everything made easy for our use. They had to undergo much trouble in folding the large sheets of paper then used, in a very precise manner, so that one end could be neatly inserted inside the other, and then the seal had to be affixed; we have now our envelopes into which to thrust our missives, securely sealed without the help of sealing-wax or wafer; our perforated stamps, so quickly torn asunder; and post cards—which device, by the way, should be made use of for transacting business matters solely, and not for private affairs—and also letter-cards. A few hints on letter-writing in general will not be out of place before speaking of the various styles proper on different occasions.

In order to make our letters pleasant to our friends, we should write as we speak, just what we have to say, and exactly in the words we should say if our correspondent were sitting by us; and then all that stiff formality, those long strings of questions, those meaningless sentences with which the mass of letters are burdened, would die a natural death. "I desire my acquaintances when they write to me," says Addison, "rather to say something which would make me wish myself with them, than make me compliments that they wished themselves with me." The Germans give strict injunctions that you should not mention yourself before you have introduced the person of your correspondent; that is, you must not use the monosyllable "I" before the pronoun "you"—a command which it would be well to issue in this country, and so put a stop to that wearisome formula of commencement, "I hope you are quite well." The handwriting should be clear, and yet not too large and bold; it should possess some character and style, but not be adorned or ornamented with fine flourishes and dashes. The minute Italian handwriting—in which the words and letters appeared to possess no individuality of their own—has now passed out of date, and a freer, nobler style has taken its place. There is a fashion in letter-paper and envelopes which is ever varying as to size and shape—sometimes small, at other times large; now oblong, now square; but one thing never alters, and that is the desirability of using good thick paper and envelopes, whatever the shape may be. Nothing looks more mean and untidy than thin sheets and envelopes of the same quality, through which the writing exhibits itself.

Some years ago the letter-paper and envelopes used for notes of invitation were of the daintiest and tiniest size; the edges were lined with gold or silver, and the most fairy-like impression in white wax fastened the missive. Now we have gone somewhat to the other extreme, and use paper and envelopes of much larger size. We are plainer too. All show and smartness is forbidden. No blue or red-edged paper; no fancifully coloured ink; no gaudily illuminated device of crest or armorial bearings is admissible. The letter-paper which is considered to show the most correct taste is of medium thickness, is finely ribbed, slightly glazed, and delicately tinted. Envelopes should match the letter-paper in all respects. A fashion prevalent with regard to envelopes is to have the address stamped across the flap; but this, to our mind, is most objectionable, and simply calculated to satisfy the incurable curiosity of servants as regards the correspondence of their employers.

The address is written or printed on one side

at the top of the first page; the monogram, or crest, when used, opposite. If on mourning paper these are in black, otherwise they should be printed in white, or *one colour only*. Letters should not be commenced very high or very low on the page, but should be nearer the top than the bottom. It is always more desirable to take a second sheet than to cross the writing, a habit which renders the reading of the letter a task, and one to which men particularly object.

The size of paper used should be according to the style of note written. Printed cards for formal invitations are now almost invariably used; but should these kinds of invitations be written, a small size—that called the "Albert"—is used.

Cards, square in shape, and white or tinted in colour, with the address stamped on them, are used for little notes and informal invitations: also, for these same purposes, small sheets of paper stamped with address and monogram, with envelopes attached—one piece forming the two—have been brought into use.

When sealing-wax is required, either red or black must be used; but we doubt if any one could be found able to seal a letter neatly except a lady or gentleman of the olden school; so little occasion there is for the art to be practised. Wafers are never allowable.

All letters to strangers and notes of formal character should as a rule be written in the third person, and must always be answered in the same way; and we trust, for the sake of the writer's reputation, that they will be better worded and less confused than the one subjoined, which was an answer sent to us by a seemingly well-educated woman, the sister of a surgeon. We put it aside as a curiosity, and now copy it verbatim; but hope that our readers will not do the same:—

> Miss B—— presents her own and her sister's and brother's joint compliments, and begs leave to say that she and they will be happy to accept the vicar's and Mrs. C——'s kind invitation on Friday evening, on the condition—which only applies though to her brother—that his presence be excused until somewhat later in the evening.
> *Thursday Morning.*

In this instance two separate notes should have been returned in answer to the invitation—which, being of a formal character, had doubtless been conveyed in that form—one for the sisters and one for the brother; or if otherwise, the reply might have been couched thus—

> The Misses and Mr. B—— have much pleasure in accepting Mr. and Mrs. C——'s kind invitation for Friday evening. Mr. B—— regrets that an engagement will prevent him from coming until later in the evening.

In certain cases, however, such as asking the character of a servant, where it is necessary to ask numerous questions and make various remarks, it is better to write in the first person even to a stranger, as the constant repetition of the names in a letter of any length becomes awkward. In that case the commencement would be "Sir" or "Madam," and the conclusion "Yours truly." To ordinary acquaintances "Yours sincerely" is the correct termination; and whatever the degree of friendship, we are inclined to think that *great* demonstrations of affection and terms of endearment are better avoided, or left only for the use of lovers. To "present compliments" is old-fashioned, and so is to "avail yourself."

An invitation to dinner is issued in the name of

the gentleman and lady. The following is the form for printed cards :—

> Mr. and Mrs. THOMPSON
> Request the pleasure of
> Mr. and Mrs. FIELD's
> company at Dinner on Saturday,
> the 9th of May, at half-past 7 o'clock.
> *Arncliffe, April 26th.*

Mr. and Mrs. FIELD accept with pleasure Mr. and Mrs. THOMPSON's kind invitation to dinner on the 9th of May.
Sunny How, April 27th.

An invitation to a ball, evening party, or an "At Home," in the name of the lady only :—

> *Mr. and Mrs. Childers.*
> Mrs. SIMPSON,
> At Home,
> Thursday, March 12th
> Music 9 o'clock.　　　　　R.S.V.P.
> 8, *Tenterden Square.*

> Mrs. LYON requests the pleasure of
> Mr. and Mrs. HARLEY's
> company on the evening of
> January the fourteenth.
> Dancing 10 o'clock.　　　　R.S.V.P.
> *The Beeches.*

Mr. and Mrs. HARLEY have much pleasure in accepting Mrs. LYON's kind invitation for the even'ng of the 14th of January.
Belle Vue, January 6th.

The following is a form of invitation sent by the parents of a Bride-elect to those friends who are not asked to be guests at the house:—

>Mr. and Mrs. HAYTER
>request the honour of
>Mr. and Mrs. MASON's
>company at the Marriage
>of their daughter Mildred,
>At St. Peter's Church, Eaton Square,
>on Thursday, April 15th,
>at 2 o'clock.

The following are two forms of invitation for a garden party:—

Mr. and Mrs. Acton.
>Mrs. EDEN,
>At Home
>The Thursdays in May,
>from 4 to 7 o'clock.

Eden Hall.   Lawn Tennis.

>Mr. and Mrs. COURTENAY
>request the pleasure of
>Mr. and Miss GREY's
>company at a Garden Party
>on Friday, the 21st June, at 4 o'clock.
>Dancing after 8

Ashmeadow.   R.S.V.P

"R. S. V. P." are the initials of the words "Répondez, s'il vous plaît." In these invitations for out-of-door parties it is always well to specify the amusements, that ladies may be dressed accordingly. For instance, archery and lawn tennis require different costumes; and unless dancing is named the guests expect to leave early.

The formal acknowledgment of inquiries after an illness, etc., is :—

Mrs. HOLMES

Returns thanks for

Mrs. HILL'S

kind inquiries.

In addressing a clergyman it is usual to put "Rev." or "Dear Sir." It is no longer customary to write "B.A." or "M.A." after his name. When the Christian name happens to be unknown, write the "Rev. —— White," not the "Rev. Mr. White."

Doctors of divinity and of medicine are thus distinguished :—"To the Rev. R. Martin, D.D." or "The Rev. Dr. Martin;" "To F. G. Hopkins, Esq., M.D.," or "Dr. Hopkins;" but in each case the former is considered the more correct.

In writing to servants it is customary to begin thus :—"To Mary Farrar—Mrs. Taylor intends returning," etc.; and to tradespeople—"Mrs. Maitland will be obliged by Mr. Scott sending her 6 lb. tea," etc.

Appended are the forms for addressing persons of different ranks, and the proper superscriptions :—

The Queen—Madam—To the Queen's Most Excellent Majesty.
Members of the Royal Family—Sir—Madam—To His or Her Royal Highness.
Archbishops—My Lord Archbishop—His Grace the Archbishop of ——
Duke—My Lord Duke—His Grace the Duke of ——
Marquis—My Lord Marquis—The Most Hon. the Marquis of ——
Earl—My Lord—The Right Hon. the Earl of ——
Viscount—My Lord—The Right Hon. the Viscount ——
Baron—My Lord—The Right Hon. the Lord F——
Bishops—My Lord Bishop—The Right Rev. the Bishop of ——

Honorary titles of "K.G.," "K.C.B.," "M.P.," etc., may be added to the name. All members of the Privy Council are addressed as "Right Hon.," and the title of "Esq." is dropped, as "The Right Hon. W. E. Gladstone, M.P."

Peeresses of all the five orders are addressed as:

Duchess—My Lady—Her Grace the Duchess of ——
Marchioness—My Lady—The Most Hon. the Marchioness of ——
Countess—My Lady—The Right Hon. the Countess of ——
Viscountess—My Lady—The Right Hon. the Viscountess of ——
Baroness—My Lady—The Right Hon. the Lady F——

Widows of peers, if the successors to the title are married:—

Her Grace the Duchess Dowager of ——
The Most Noble the Marchioness Dowager of ——

The younger sons and daughters of dukes and marquises, and the daughters of dukes, marquises, and earls, are styled lords and ladies.

Younger sons of earls and younger sons and daughters of viscounts and barons are styled, in writing, "The Hon." Baronets, in order to distinguish them from knights, are addressed thus: "Sir H. Grey, Bart."

CHAPTER V.

VISITING.

The Use of "Calling"—Occasions when Calls should be paid—The Card Case and its Contents—Ceremonies of Calls—Cake and Wine—Visits—Length of Visits—Conduct when Staying in a Friend's House—Gratuities to Servants.

> "Well-dressed, well-bred, well-carriag'd,
> Is ticket good enough to pass us readily
> Through every door."
> *Cowper.*

THE ceremony of paying calls has been ridiculed and derided during the course of many, many years as meaningless, useless, and stupid; but it is still in existence, and is as much practised as ever. Visits of form, of which most people complain, and yet to which most people submit, are absolutely necessary—being, in fact, the basis on which that great structure, society, mainly rests. You cannot invite people to your house, however often you may have met them elsewhere, until you have first called upon them in a formal manner, and they have returned the visit. It is a kind of safeguard against any acquaintances which are thought to be undesirable. If you do not wish to continue the friendship, you discontinue to call, and that is considered as an intimation of such intentions, and therefore no further advances are made by them. But it would be considered very bad manners, and very uncourteous behaviour, not to return a call in the first instance. Men do not, as a rule, pay these visits of ceremony; and it would appear that they have always shirked their duties in this respect as much as possible, judging from an allusion made to this failing by a writer of the last century, who says: "It has grown to be the fashion among men to treat the business of visiting with great disrespect. They look upon it as a mere female recreation, and beneath the dignity of their superior natures. Yet, notwithstanding their contempt, and the odious name of 'gadding' which they have given it, I do not find that they fail in their appearance at any of our assemblies, or that they are better able to shut themselves up in their own houses when there is anything to be seen or done abroad."

There is something to be said in defence of the men: their days are occupied with other and more serious business; their evenings can be given to their friends, and so they thus escape the monotony of calling, and yet are allowed to enjoy the various festive gatherings—provided, of course, that their cards have duly represented their owners at the houses of their acquaintances.

There are a great many occasions when calls should be paid. There are calls congratulatory, calls of condolence, and calls of courtesy. A bride is called upon shortly after entering her new home. Her parents receive the congratulations immediately the engagement is announced, and after the marriage has taken place. A mother also on the birth of a child—indeed, it is usual, when any cause for congratulation arises, that friends should at once offer their good wishes in person. On the other hand, should sorrow or any domestic calamity befall any of our acquaintances, condolences and sympathy should be offered—not immediately, as in the other cases; but sufficient time should be allowed to the family before we venture to ask to see them. There should be no hasty intrusion upon their trouble and grief. To ensure this respect, it has become the custom to "return thanks for kind inquiries," and after these have been received, then the call may be paid.

Lastly, there are calls general. These are made in the country upon people when they first come into the neighbourhood; and in a town—where every one eyes askance a stranger—after an introduction has been made on the first occasion through some common friend; these formal visits should always be returned within three or four days. After receiving any particular hospitality, such as a dinner or ball, it is necessary to call or merely to leave cards at the door within the few following days. The hours for calling are between three and six o'clock p.m. No call should be paid before luncheon, unless on a very familiar friend.

Cards must be left on all occasions of a formal character. A lady leaves her own and two of her husband's—one is intended for the gentleman of the house and one for the lady. If a call is made upon a guest staying at the house, a card is also left for her. A lady when leaving cards for her husband must place them upon the hall table, and not leave them in the drawing-room on her departure, as was the custom. Should the lady upon whom you call not be at home, you turn down one corner of the cards, which signifies that you have called personally. Cards with inquiries should be left at the door; the post is a permissible channel for the transmission of these where the distance is inconveniently great. When you arrive in town you call and leave your card as an intimation that you are in the neighbourhood, thus acting the reverse of what is considered proper when in the country, where the rule is that the stranger waits until called upon. In towns, and more particularly that vast Babylon, London, people cannot be aware of the movements and arrivals of their friends, as is the case in the country; so that unless an intimation of this kind reached them, the town friend would be quite ignorant of the proximity of his country friend.

The cards of our grandfathers and grandmothers wore a very important look—they were of large size, very stiff, very highly glazed, and had the names written in a series of flourishes. Ours are much less ostentatious, plain cards, the gentleman's smaller than the lady's, with name and address printed in an ordinary style. Married people often have their names together on one card, as—

Mr. and Mrs. JOHNSON.

4 Elkam Place.

Unmarried daughters have their names placed under that of their mother—

Mrs. BENSON.
Miss BENSON.

The Cedars,
   Parminster.

Merely honorary or official designations are omitted, except on cards used for visits of a purely official character.

The initials P.D.A. (*Pour dire adieu*) or P.P.C. (*Pour prendre congé*) are written on the right-hand corner of the card when a call is made for the purpose of leave-taking, such as that paid before a long absence from the neighbourhood.

"Wedding cards," which formerly used to present a very smart and elaborate appearance—thin satin cards, with broad silver edges, tied together with silver thread, and enclosed in an envelope to match, and fastened down by a silver wafer—are never sent nowadays.

It has been remarked that, notwithstanding the copiousness of the English language, there is only one word for the different times which are occupied by a visit. People can find no term to express their design of staying fifteen days at a house different from that which signifies fifteen minutes. The would-be reformer goes on to say:—"When a fine lady, having a new-fashioned suit of clothes, finds it necessary to call upon forty or fifty of her friends in one day, I am for an abridgment of the word, and would call it a *vis*. When a gentleman or lady intends taking a family dinner with country friends, or a dish of tea with a town one, I would have that called a *visit*. But when a person purposes spending some days, weeks, or months at a house, I would call that a *visitation*." Instead of abridging the word, which is always an unwise thing to do, we have found another word altogether for the short stay of a few minutes in another person's house, and now we speak of "a call," and "a visit" means spending at least a night from home.

No call of a purely formal nature should be of long duration—certainly not more than a quarter of an hour. If you find callers already there, do not outstay them, but leave the house even sooner than you otherwise would have done. The lady when receiving her friends should introduce them to each other. She rises to receive each visitor as they enter the room, and, if possible, offers a chair near to her own to the last comer. If there are gentlemen in the room, they also rise when other people enter; but the ladies, should there be any present, do not leave their seats. Of course very much depends upon the degree of intimacy which exists; if this be very great, it will naturally modify much of the formality absolutely necessary in other cases. There is a picture, drawn in the fifteenth century, of a room full of callers, which looks very formal and stiff. A bench is round the room, close to the wall, and on it are seated all the ladies present, with their hands folded on their knees, while the gentlemen are seated on stools, and wear their hats. It requires considerable art, and I might almost say presence of mind, to entertain alone a great many callers at one time. The lady who receives them should try and converse with all; no one in particular should engross her attention. This is no easy matter to perform well and gracefully. When callers rise to take their leave, the lady of the house rings the bell that the servant may be at hand to open the hall door. If the gentleman of the house be present, he escorts the lady to the hall door and puts her into her carriage. "Good-bye" is the form of leave-taking, and not "Good-morning." A gentleman should bring his hat and stick into the room, and keep them in his hands, unless anything requires him to set his hands at liberty: he then places them on the floor. A married lady of our acquaintance, ignorant of this little piece of etiquette, was quite offended with a gentleman who called upon her for taking his hat and stick into *her* drawing-room. "Why did he not leave them in the hall?" said she; "there was a hat-stand for his accommodation."

Many ladies adopt the plan of always being at home on stated afternoons, which are written on their visiting-cards, thus, "At home on Thursdays;" "At home the first and third Monday in the month."

In country places, where people lived miles apart, it was the time-honoured custom to offer wine and cake to every caller. At one time even distance was not considered; hospitality was dispensed to every comer, whether they were next-door neighbours or not. Here is an amusing instance of the strictness with which this rule is still observed in some parts.

A very splendid mansion was lately erected quite close to the house of my friends, therefore they thought it would be but a neighbourly courtesy to call upon the new comers. They accordingly one day crossed the road, ascended a flight of steps which led to a massive portal, and, having waited some time for admission, were at last invited to walk in by some one who did not match the rest of the house in appearance. Across a noble hall, over a marble floor, and into a magnificent drawing-room they were ushered, and there left for some time to admire the splendour around them while the good woman of the house, it was presumed, put on her best bib and tucker. By-and-bye the mistress appeared, resplendent in silks and lace—an imposing spectacle until the tongue gave utterance, and then what a contrast between the refinement of all the surrounding objects and the refinement of her speech! The lady began at once to communicate her domestic troubles: at present they were without servants; but Mr. —— had gone into Wales, and he would "leet" on a good one there, no doubt. In the midst of these confidences the door slowly opened, and then a tray appeared, on which rested cake and wine. The hand and arm which supported it were alone visible. The lady arose, and, taking it from the mysterious hand, carried it to the table, and commenced dispensing her hospitality.

It is considered bad manners for the lady of the house to keep her callers in "durance vile"—that is to say, for her not to go at once into the room where they have been ushered. Sometimes one calls at a house, and, having been shown into a room, has had to wait patiently or otherwise for the tardy appearance of the mistress. Whisperings are plainly heard, then consultations, then steps going stealthily up-stairs and as quietly descending, and finally the lady of the house appears in a different costume from that she had worn a quarter of an hour before. Profuse apologies invariably fall from her lips—"I am so sorry to have kept you waiting," &c. But, my dear lady, apologies, however numerous, will never make up for want of good manners; and therefore when the next caller honours you, go to her as you are, and repress the desire to exhibit your last new dress.

On the other hand, the visitors will, it is to be hoped, refrain from bringing either dogs or children. The former are apt to do a great deal of mischief in overturning things, and require the constant attention of their owner, which interrupts conversation; and the latter, besides often hearing much that they should not, are apt to make awkward remarks, and are often as mischievous amongst china and nick-nacks as the canine pet.

When you call with a letter of introduction—which, by the way, when given in the first instance, should not be sealed—it is usual to leave your card and the letter, and not go in, as, should you do so, you place the lady of the house in a dilemma. Your name does not enlighten her as to who you may be, and she cannot very well read the letter in your presence, as in that case she could not entertain you. The gentleman or lady to whom the letter is addressed should at once send an invitation, and show hospitality in some form to the friend of their friend. And now we will turn to "visitations;" but before entering into details, let us say a word of warning to the young or unmarried persons. They, and more especially the gentler portion of that community, often make mistakes by prolonging their stay at a friend's house over a much longer period of time than was first mentioned or thought of by either party; they turn visits into visitations.

Young girls have little to occupy them in their own homes, or perhaps they have too much for their liking; however that may be, they receive an invitation from a friend to spend a week or two, and the week or two merges into a month or two. They are aware that time is gliding on; but it is a pleasant existence. Amusements are provided; there are no cares nor troubles to vex and worry either mind or body; and they are loth to make the required effort. A feeble declaration is uttered by them; but directly the hostess says—as politeness requires—"Oh, must you go?" or "Can't you stay longer with us?" the young visitor catches at the words, and settles comfortably down again, and prolongs her sojourn. "Never outstay your welcome" is an old but a good saying; and we have very often heard the remark made, "I cannot (or shall not) ask Miss So-and-so; she always stays so long when she comes, and one never knows when she will go." If you are not well acquainted with those who invite you, and particularly if they are people who keep a great deal of company, two or three days is the usual time. Of course the time you stay depends very much, too, on the size of your party. It is better when inviting your friends to specify the length: "I shall be glad if you will spend a week with us." The hostess should take particular care to be at home when her guests arrive, and ready to receive and welcome them. Nothing gives a greater chill than a cold or a tardy welcome, and nothing gives more pleasure than a cheerful, prompt, and hearty greeting.

> "There is a certain hospitable air
> In a friend's house that tells me I am welcome:
> The porter opens to me with a smile,
> The yard dog wags his tail, the servant runs,
> Beats up the cushions, spreads the couch, and says,
> 'Sit down, good sir,' ere I can say I'm weary."

"There is," says Washington Irving, "an emanation from the heart in genuine hospitality which cannot be described, but is immediately felt, and which puts the stranger at once at his ease." The manner of greeting is not so free now as in olden days. Then it was in deeds as well as words. It is still customary for great and dear friends and relations to salute one another with the kiss of peace; but this is anything but a universal mode of salutation, at least in demure and proper England. In France and Germany, on the contrary, the inhabitants go to the other extreme, and men kiss one another in public and in private. That this form of greeting was once more *à la mode* in our country than it now is we learn from the remarks made by three foreign travellers. Chalcondylas, a Greek, who visited our island four or five centuries ago, was highly surprised, delighted, and edified with this way of procedure. He says, "As for English females and children, their customs are liberal in the extreme. When a visitor calls at a friend's house, his first act is to kiss his friend's wife." Nicander Nicius also adverts to this osculatory practice; and Erasmus, the staid Dutchman, becomes quite lively when expatiating upon this subject. He writes, "The English have a custom which can never be sufficiently commended. On your arrival you are welcomed with kisses, on your departure you are sent off with kisses; if you return the embraces are repeated; wherever you meet you are greeted with a kiss; whichever way you turn there is nothing but kissing."

A hostess will make all the arrangements in her power to provide for the pleasure and amusement of her guests; and the guests in return must not be unmindful of what is incumbent on them. They should readily fall into all the plans that are made for their entertainment, and try to assimilate their ways to those of the household of which they are members for the time being, even in what may seem to them trivial matters. They should not expect the attention either of their host or hostess during the morning hours. Breakfast and luncheon do not require a punctual attendance, as at those meals it is not considered impolite to begin at the stated hour, whether all the guests have assembled or not. But not to be in the drawing-room when dinner is announced, to absent yourself after dinner, or to make any plans irrespective of your entertainers, are grave offences against social law. The time of retiring for the night is intimated in various ways; a not unusual sign is the appearance of a tray with wine, soda-water, and biscuits, after partaking of which there is a distribution of candlesticks amongst the ladies, who retire to their own apartments; and the gentlemen also vacate the drawing-room, and some, perhaps, adjourn to the smoking-room.

Fees or no fees? No definite determination has yet been arrived at with regard to this often-discussed question of giving money to servants. In some few houses the owners have placed cards in their visitors' bed-rooms, requesting them not to give gratuities; but servants, like railway porters, look out for their *douceurs*. All those who have rendered a guest any assistance look for an acknowledgment, and their hands are always on the alert when the moment of your departure arrives, to receive and close upon the gold or silver coin deposited therein.

A lady gives to the maid who has assisted her with her toilet, and the housemaid. A gentleman remembers the valet, butler, coachman, gamekeeper—any and all who have rendered him any service, and the donations are according to the wealth of the donor; but, as a rule, the men-servants in *large* houses expect gold. These gratuities are really a great tax upon people's purses; and the question whether to accept an invitation is often decided in the negative by the thought of the expenses entailed, not by railway tickets and cabs, but by the men and the maids.

CHAPTER VI.

THE TOILET.—DRESS, NEATNESS, AND SUITABILITY.

Style of Dress appropriate for different Occasions—A Christening—When Paying Calls—At Garden Parties—Picnics—The Seaside—Morning Dress—Dinner and Ball Dresses—Jewellery—Bride's Costume; Bridesmaids'—The Guests at a Wedding—Mourning—Man's Dress—As a Bridegroom—At Garden Parties—Seaside—" Full Dress "—Jewellery—The Hat and Gloves.

> " And now the toilet stands displayed."
> *Pope.*

> " Come, tailor, let us see't.
> Oh mercy ! what masking stuff is here ?
> What's this ? A sleeve ?"
> *Shakespeare.*

As Dr. Doran remarks, " Man is the only animal born without being provided with a necessary costume ; plants die that man may live, and animals are skinned that the lords of the creation may be covered." It is therefore essential that the toilet should be a matter for thought and consideration for every one.

Now this chapter is not intended to be a dissertation upon fashion ; that I leave to the dressmakers' monthly periodicals, for

> "Our dress still varying,
> Nor to forms confined,
> Shifts like the sand, the sport
> Of every wind."

I shall simply show what is the style and character of dress appropriate for wear on different occasions.

I agree with Dr. Watts, that

> "It is in good manners, and not in good dress,
> That the truest gentility lies;"

but still I think the two go very much together, and that dress has a certain effect on the character and manners. Most people hold that the reverse of this is true, and that a person's dress is influenced by his character. Probably each has an influence on the other; but be that as it may, an ill-dressed man is never so much at his ease as a well-dressed man, and I believe that mean and shabby clothing has an unconscious hold on the mind.

> "Costly thy habit as thy purse can buy,
> But not expressed in fancy—rich, not gaudy;
> For the apparel oft proclaims the man."

I have elsewhere protested against "best" rooms and "company" manners, and would here remark that the habit of being particular in our attire only when we appear before "company" is a bad one, and an "ill habit has the force of an ill fate." The eyes of those who form our home circle should never be distressed by an untidy appearance. Circumstances may forbid our garments being either rich or costly, but neatness and simple elegance can always be shown in every dress and at every season. "My wife appears decent enough in her apparel to those who visit us in an afternoon; but in the morning she is quite another figure," writes a complainant.

There is no easier method by which to detect the real lady from the sham one than by noticing her style of dress. Vulgarity is readily distinguished, however costly and fashionable the habiliments may be, by the breach of certain rules of harmony and fitness. No one, perhaps, can dress perfectly without a genius for it, but every one can avoid vulgarity and slovenliness, and attain the average standard of gentility. Neatness we have spoken of as a requisite element, and another and all-important one is suitability—suitability as to various times and seasons—suitability as to age.

A dress which would look perfectly well on one occasion will appear out of place and vulgar on another. A costume in which a young woman looks bewitching makes an older one look absurd and ridiculous.

Our neighbours on the other side of the Channel, who are always held up to us as models of taste, are very particular in these points—neatness and suitability—and we must own that an Englishwoman rarely presents an appearance as elegant as a Frenchwoman, even though the attire of the former may be gorgeous, and that of the latter simple and plain in the extreme. The French excel, too, in the assortment and harmonising of colours. They never dream of decking themselves in all the hues of the rainbow; one, or at the most two colours predominate in their whole dress; and whatever the colours chosen, they are selected with a view to suit the complexion of the wearer. Alas and alack! for Englishwomen in respect to these matters. Here, you see one with drab face and drab dress; there, one bedizened like a harlequin; some in silks and satins, lace and jewels, when the occasion demands that they should be plainly clad in woollens and cambric; mothers and grandmothers affecting a style of juvenility which would look charming on their descendants, but ill-becomes their grey heads and wrinkled brows. The old lady I saw at a college concert, who had placed on the back of her grey-haired head a bunch of brown hair, and considered that a sufficient ornament without the addition of cap or lappet; and the one I met at a ball, attired in white satin, with her bare seventy-year-old neck and shoulders powdered and devoid of scarf or shawl, forgot the fact that the aping of juvenility "multiplies the wrinkles of old age, and makes its decay more conspicuous."

But let us proceed to review the various styles of dress proper for different occasions.

The dress worn by a mother at her infant's christening and her own churching should be plain and neat, but handsome and substantial. There is an entry in King Edward II.'s "Household Book" to the following effect: "To the Queen's tailor was delivered five pieces of white velvet, for the making thereof a certain robe against the churching of the Queen after the birth of her son." A dress of silken material will look more in accordance with the occasion than one of thin texture.

The costume for paying calls when on foot differs from that which should be worn for the same purpose when driving in a carriage. In the former case it will be of a much plainer character. It may be light or dark, according to the season; but it must not be gay, and not have anything about it to attract attention, but be like that of the lady of whom Dr. Johnson said that he was sure she was well dressed, because he could not remember anything that she had on.

Carriage dress has much more licence. Handsome costumes, made of rich silken materials, flowery or feathery bonnets and lace sunshades, which would look quite out of place when walking, are suitable when driving. For some years black gloves were universally worn at all times and seasons, and with every style of dress. Their place has been taken by tan-coloured gloves, which are worn with evening as well as with morning attire. Those made of soft, dull suède kid are selected for evening wear in preference to the thicker glossy kid. When paying calls, gloves of a shade harmonising in colour with the dress are usually worn. All gloves are long, and are fastened by many buttons, the number of which varies from six on those worn out of doors to twenty on those worn with evening dress. Bracelets and bangles of gold or silver are worn over the glove.

The toilet for garden parties, bazaars, flower-shows, &c., is of a brighter, gayer fashion, and affords room for the display of much taste and elegance. Young women attire themselves in delicately tinted fine materials — materials which have a refinement, beauty, and softness characteristic of those whom they are designed to embellish, but quite distinctive from those worn in the ball-room. These costumes are made as effective and coquettish as possible—everything that will add to the gaiety, without passing the limits of morning attire, is permissible, and the whole is crowned by a bonnet or hat of like description. The elder ladies should wear silks or some handsome material, richly trimmed with lace, a foreign shawl or lace mantle, and bonnets, not hats, whether in town or country.

Costumes for picnics, excursions, and for seaside wear should be of a useful character. Nothing looks worse at these times than a thin, flimsy fabric, which will split and tear at every turn, or a faded, shabby silk; and nothing looks better than some strong material, either one that will wash or otherwise, but of such a description that it will look almost as well at the end of a day's hard wear as at the beginning.

Yachting dresses are generally made of serge or tweed, as those materials are unspoilable by sea air and water, and at the same time possess warmth and durability.

The dresses worn by lawn-tennis players have various distinctive features. Wool, much or little, should in some measure form the material, for health's sake, as a preventive of chills being taken; therefore cashmere, serge, and flannel are chosen. As the dress should not be heavy, fineness of wool and lightness of weight of material have to be considered. The bodice is usually made full, and the skirt is short, and not burdened with many frills and flounces. But within these boundary lines, prettiness and embellishments can be introduced —combinations of colours, bright ribbons, and various other adornments will give the dress an attractive appearance. A receptacle for the tennis balls is sometimes part of the player's costume. An ornamental and useful one should be arranged, made of the same material as the dress. Its form can be that of a flat pocket, or a bag, suspended from the waist. Hats of every variety are worn, of all shapes and sizes. They should in some degree suit the rest of the costume in style and appearance.

And next of indoor dresses.

A lady's morning dress should be simple and refined, and suited to the time of day. No old "company" gown should exhibit itself and its shabbiness in the morning light, but a dress fresh as the morn itself; as inexpensive as you please, but clean and appropriate it must be. Lace, unless of a thick description, is not worn with morning attire. Honiton and Brussels would be quite out of place. Neither is much jewellery consistent; plain gold and silver ornaments are permissible, but never precious stones, except in rings.

When visiting at a friend's house the morning dress may be of a slightly superior style; for instance, a white embroidered dress may be worn where one of coloured cotton would be used at home, or a velveteen instead of a serge one; but remember that "great external display is generally said to be employed to hide internal vulgarity," and we know of nothing which evinces not only greater want of taste, but also ignorance of the habits of good society, than smartness in morning attire, and especially a lavish display of jewellery.

Again, a dinner dress differs from that worn at a ball, although they both may be termed "full dress." For the former occasions silks and satins, velvets and brocades, are the materials chosen, and are trimmed with lace. The neck and arms of the wearer are now generally covered, excepting at a specially "full-dress" dinner; the bodice is made high, but open in front, and the sleeves reach the elbow.

Of late years young women have so arranged

their hair that extra adornments have not been in much favour—a jewelled ornament placed according to fancy, a decorative comb, or bow of ribbon, arranged in the manner most becoming to the shape of the head, or the style in which the hair is dressed, are employed. Older ladies wear caps composed of flowers, of feathers, of pearls, of fine lace or combinations of lace with one or more of the above-named.

In the ball-room nothing but complete full dress should be worn. For young people dresses of fabrics of those textures which do not look thick and heavy are chosen, such as surah silk, tulle, net, gauze, and the like, trimmed with lace and flowers. The bodice is made low, with short sleeves; or cut open in front and at the back, with shoulder-straps, and sleeves to the elbow. Extremes in the forms of the dresses worn on these occasions attract observation, but not admiration.

The flowers worn on these occasions are generally artificial, because natural ones so soon fall to pieces from the heat of the room and the movements of the dancers.

The dress of the chaperons should be similar in character to that worn at a dinner. Jewellery is generally worn in sets; ornaments never look so well if pieces of different sets are displayed together; that is to say, if diamonds are in the brooch, a necklet of pearls and earrings set with emeralds would not look well if worn on the same occasion. All the ornaments should match in character as much as possible, but variety is allowed in the matter of bracelets.

The bride's costume now demands attention. Formerly magnificence and costliness were studied before elegance and grace. We flatter ourselves that in our time bridal attire is more worthy of admiration, though not as gorgeous as of yore. History tells us that the bridal dress of one lady—a royal one, it is true, but subjects always follow as closely as they may the fashions set them by their sovereigns—was composed of velvet and cloth of gold, and the weight of it was sixty pounds! Brides of the present day are dressed entirely in white, unless for a second marriage, when it is usual to choose some delicate colour for the dress, such as silver grey, pearl-white, or dove-colour, and also to wear a bonnet instead of the virgin veil. The dress of a young bride is made of soft-textured silk or satin or brocade, trimmed with flowers and rich white lace, and a large veil of the same description of lace as that on the dress. This is placed on the head so as to fall on to the skirt of the dress, equally behind and in front. The wearing of the veil appears to have originated with the Anglo-Saxons, whose custom it was to perform the ceremony of marriage under a square piece of cloth, which was held at each corner by a tall man over the bridegroom and the bride, for the purpose of concealing her blushes. If the bride had been married before, the veil was dispensed with.

Some twenty or thirty years ago it was correct to wear "full dress" at a wedding; that is, the bride's dress was made low, with short sleeves, and the bridegroom wore an evening suit. Now, morning attire is proper for gentlemen, and the bride's costume too is much more simple. A wreath of white flowers is worn under the veil, white gloves and shoes, and a bouquet composed entirely of white flowers. Any great display of jewellery is in bad taste, and the little that may be allowed should not be florid or elaborate. A set of pearls looks well, or something of the same plain and simple character.

There is more variety in bridesmaids' dresses than in that of a bride. A picturesque costume is often chosen which combines two colours, or is made entirely of one shade of colour. The hats or bonnets are often composed of the same material as the dress, or else of that which trims it. The flowers worn are generally those which would be naturally blooming at that season. Sometimes veils of plain tulle are worn, and wreaths take the place of bonnets. When this is the case the veil does not fall over the face, like that of the bride, but entirely down the back. All the bridesmaids are dressed alike, and their bouquets are composed of coloured flowers. Neither the bride nor her maids, when veils are worn, wear anything over their shoulders except their dresses and veils.

The young ladies who do not hold the office of bridesmaids should choose some dainty dress material. If children are present at a wedding, girls look the best in costumes of white or pale colours, and little boys in some fancy costume, or in velvet suits made after the fashion of the Royal pages-in-waiting of bygone days.

The older guests at a wedding should choose some handsome, rich material, and have it trimmed with either white or black lace. Over their shoulders should be worn a lace mantle or one of silk or satin, and their bonnets trimmed with feathers and flowers.

Formerly mourning was worn both for a longer period and of a much deeper character than is usual at the present time. Two years was not considered too long a time for a near relative, such as father or mother. Now, one year for relations of that degree, and six months for uncles, aunts, or cousins, is the general time. In these days it is considered better taste to wear plainer and less heavy, expensive, and ostentatious habiliments than heretofore. Widows wear their weeds, which consist of crape dress, large black silk cloak, crape bonnet and veil, plain muslin collar and broad cuffs (or "weepers," as they are termed), and "widow's cap," usually for a year, and then discontinue the particular signs which distinguish a widow, such as cap, weepers, and veil, and wear ordinary mourning for as long a time as they may wish. Deep mourning is considered to be woollen fabrics and crape. What is called "second mourning" is dull black silk or cashmere, with or without crape. The third stage, which is called "half mourning," is black and white. Complimentary mourning is black without crape.

Of course it will be thought that there cannot be much to say about men's toilets, since they are supposed never to think about dress, nor talk about it, and rarely to change their fashions. I have said very little about them yet, it is true; but had I space at my command I could write pages to show how in every age the art of dress has been one of the leading studies of the masculine mind.

An old Anglo-Saxon chronicler writes that the young men of his day were more foppish and vain of their appearance than the ladies, and to prove his words he adduces the following reasons: that they used to comb their hair every day, bathed every Saturday, often changed their clothes, and used many other such frivolous means for setting off the beauty of their persons! Then we read that in Henry I.'s time men vied with women in the length of their locks, and wherever these were wanting they put on false tresses. During the time of James I. the beaux wore long love-locks, and sometimes stuck flowers behind their ears; and a certain Earl of Pembroke, a man far from being an effeminate character, is represented as wearing earrings! Tales might be told of the wrought nightcaps, which were embroidered in gold and silk for physicians, and in black and white for the clergy. Pepys, in his quaint, open, simple way, thus discloses to us the vanity of the sex in his day, for he not only jots down the different costumes noticed by him as worn by his fair acquaintances, but a great many pages are devoted to descriptions of his own apparel. Here is one out of the many like passages with which his Diary abounds:—

"Oct. 30.—£43 worse than I was last month. But it hath chiefly arisen from my laying out in clothes for myself and wife, viz.: for her about £12, and for myself £55 or thereabouts. Having made myself a velvet cloak, two new cloth shirts, both black and plain; a new shag gown, trimmed with gold buttons and twist; with a new hat and silk tops for my legs; two periwigs, whereof the one cost me £3, and the other thirty shillings. These not worn yet, but begin next month, God willing."

The dress of that day must have added greatly to the splendour and gaiety of the *coup d'œil* on all occasions, while the sombre, tame appearance of ours decidedly detracts from it.

The dress of Richard Cœur de Lion as a bridegroom was a satin tunic of a rose colour, belted round the waist; a mantle of striped silver tissue, brocaded with silver crescents; and on his head a rose-coloured bonnet, brocaded in gold with figures of animals. The bridegroom of fifty years ago appeared in light-blue tail-coat, with gold buttons, white waistcoat, knee-breeches, shoes and buckles, the ordinary evening suit of that period. The bridegroom of to-day is dressed in morning attire —dark frock-coat, with waistcoat, and trousers of some fashionable shade, and scarf or tie of a tint which harmonises with the rest of the suit. The other gentlemen present at a wedding wear the same style of dress. At a *fête champêtre* given by Queen Mary, the gentlemen who attended Princess Elizabeth were attired in russet damask and blue satin, with caps of silver cloth and blue plumes. At garden parties in town the men wear frock-coats, either dark-blue, grey, or black, white waistcoats, light trousers, and silk hats.

For seaside and country use, a complete suit of dark-blue serge or mixed tweed is found the most suitable wear.

The present style of evening dress has been much abused as so closely resembling that worn by waiters. The black tail-coat, waistcoat (sometimes white), and trousers, and white tie, present a sombre not to say a gloomy appearance, and furnish no scope for variety from year to year, except in the shape and cut.

Having described the different styles of men's dress, it may be as well to remark that what has been said in the former part of the chapter about "suitability" equally applies to their costumes as to that of ladies. For instance, when it is said that a tweed suit is worn in the country, it must not be supposed that that costume is there suitable for every occasion and at all times of the day. On some occasions neither the tweed costume nor the evening dress suit would be appropriate, but the intermediate dress should be worn—a suit such as is usually donned on Sundays either in town or country—black frock-coat, coloured trousers, and dark tie or scarf. No attempt should ever be made to combine morning and evening dress; they should always be quite distinct the one from the other.

It is not considered good taste for a man to wear much jewellery. A plain, handsome ring, studs, and sleeve-links, a watch-chain without pendants, will always look more seemly than a great display of elaborate ornaments.

Men should wear gloves in the street, or at a ball; when paying a call, driving, riding, and in church; but not usually in the country, and not at a dinner. But of all the various articles which compose the male attire, there is perhaps not one which has so much character and expression as the head-dress. "A neat, well-brushed, short-napped gentlemanly hat, put on with a certain air, gives a look of distinction and respectability to the whole exterior."

CHAPTER VII.

MARRIAGE.

"Things to be thought of"—Interview with Father-in-Law—Engagement Ring—Wedding Presents—Etiquette of Courtship—The Bridesmaids—The Licence and Banns—Bridegroom's Presents to Bride and her Maids—Day before the Wedding—Wedding Day—The Ceremony—The Breakfast—The Departure—Amusements for the rest of the Day.

> " And all went merry as a marriage bell."
> *Byron.*
>
> "—— she look'd, she blush'd consent;
> He grasped her hand, to church they went."

If all courtships and weddings were conducted in the very summary and abrupt manner described in the above lines, this chapter would be a superfluous one; but, in truth, there is a multitude of things to be done at the time of an event of this kind, and a thousand preparations to be made beforehand. Indeed, a wedding necessitates much thought and labour and numberless arrangements, from the time when the happy day is fixed upon up to the very last minute of the day itself. The wear and tear of mind is indescribable, more particularly to the members of the bride-elect's family. The trousseau—whom to ask to be bridesmaids—the guests to be invited to the wedding and to the wedding-feast—who ought to be invited to stay in the house during the time—how to provide for visitors who cannot be so accommodated—the perplexing question whether hospitality is to take the form of breakfast, luncheon, or afternoon tea—the amusement of the guests for the rest of the day—these and all the thousand and one details consequent on them are no light burden to support. Of course, in one sense, it is all a pleasant kind of "worry."

From time immemorial weddings have been considered by most nations to be occasions for feasting and rejoicing. This idea has been carried out in different ways, but all agree that happiness and merriment should be the prevailing sentiments. I have heard of but one exception. Madame Pfeiffer tells us that there is an Eastern country wherein the custom is for the bride, after the marriage ceremony—which is performed in the forenoon—to sit for the remainder of the day in a corner of the room with her face to the wall. She is not allowed to answer any one whatever, still less is she permitted to speak herself. This silence, it appears, is intended to typify the sorrow of the bride at changing her condition.

But there are several preliminaries to consider before speaking of the eventful day. Having wooed and won the faire ladye, the happy suitor has next to undergo the dreaded ordeal of asking her father's or her guardian's consent. It is the fashion in novels to depict all fathers on these occasions as stern, with adamantine hearts. In real everyday life they are to be met with here and there, and exist, we must suppose, on purpose to prove in those cases the truth of the old adage, that "the course of true love never does run smoothe."

It is said that in the olden times of our country,

the women made the advances, and often became the suitors; but it is not upon record whether they asked the consent of their future fathers-in-law.

In cases where the lady possesses a large fortune, or where the gentleman has little besides love to offer, it is considered the more honourable course for him to seek the parents' consent before the daughter's, and to ask their permission to lay his heart at her feet. However this may be, the first interview between two men in this position must perforce be an uncomfortable one. It is a father's duty to go thoroughly into the subject—to examine future prospects, to weigh the purse, to speak of deeds—not "doughty deeds," but parchment ones —and settlements, and dower. All these practical matters—matters so essential to the future happiness and well-being of the young couple—must be spoken of and talked over, in order that there be no rash vows—no need for disagreement in the future.

Nervous, timid suitors often try to evade this trying ordeal by writing their petition instead of preferring it personally, which is but a weak mode of procedure, we are inclined to think; as should the consent be given it is only a postponement of the inevitable; and should it be withheld the chance is lost of trying persuasive eloquence, or of offering further explanations—for "to write is to speak beyond hearing, and none stand by to explain."

The ceremony of betrothal, which still exists in many lands, is no longer observed in ours. In Holland all the friends and neighbours of the engaged couple assemble and celebrate it by an extensive consumption of *briudsuker* (bridal sugar) and *briudstranen* (bridal tears), as the spiced wine drunk on that occasion is figuratively named. In England it was once the custom to break in half a gold or silver coin, in token of a verbal contract of marriage and promise of love, each party treasuring a half. Now it is the fashion for the *fiancé* to give his *fiancée* a ring of a plain though handsome description, one that can be worn afterwards as a guard to the wedding-ring. There is a superstition forbidding the ring to be set either with opals or emeralds—the former because they denote change, the latter jealousy. The Gypsy ring, a broad band with the stones (diamonds, pearls, rubies, or turquoises) let in, as it were, in a circle round the ring, is a favourite and pretty choice. The engagement ring of the Princess of Wales was one of this description, and the stones were so selected and set that their initial letters formed the name of "Bertie," that being the pet name of the royal bridegroom-elect. If a simple inexpensive ring be required, a band of gold, chased, but without stones, may be used. The engagement ring is worn on the third finger of the left hand, by itself, until the wedding ring is placed on the same finger, when the engagement ring acts as its keeper.

When the engagement takes place, the relations of the happy man should immediately express a wish to be introduced to his *fiancée*, if they are strangers to her, in order that they may welcome her as a future member of their family. If they live in the immediate neighbourhood, they call upon her and her parents; if at a distance, they invite her to pay them a visit, when her lover accompanies her and introduces her to his family.

The engagement should be announced to all

relations and friends, who should at once offer their congratulations to the bride-elect and to her parents, either personally or by letter.

Directly people hear of the contemplated marriage of an acquaintance, the first thought which crosses their mind is, "What shall we give them?" —a most difficult question to answer, and one which is the cause of much cogitation to the anxious and bewildered donor.

It would seem as if people's ideas always run in the same grooves in this matter, to judge from the little variety displayed in the selection. We have heard of as many as a dozen fish-slices finding their way into the young couple's keeping; and as to butter-knives, they are apt to muster as strong as pigeon-pies at a picnic. What a pity it is that there is not a committee of friends appointed to arrange this important business! Much perplexity and doubt might thus be saved. Some people avoid the difficulty by sending a sum of money to the bride-elect, to be spent by her on what she wishes. This plan is becoming very general.

But what are the affianced ones doing all this time? Not appearing in public without a chaperon, it is to be hoped. The office of chaperon, though an honorary one, is generally deemed to be a laborious post, and on these occasions it is— we were going to say, a disagreeable one. At any rate, it cannot be agreeable to be in the position of being one too many, and where you are not wanted. This third person who plays propriety is also known by the name of "Gooseberry." The origin of this term is now quite forgotten. Perhaps Burns explains it when he says—

> "It's hardly in a body's power
> To keep at times from being sour."

Lovers should not make a practice of absenting themselves, or of being so entirely absorbed with each other as to completely ignore or neglect others whose company they may be in. Neither is it considered good manners to display demonstrative affection continually, or publicly. "All frothy tendernesses and amorous boilings-over are insults on and affronts to company," says Swift. It is to be feared that very often "we that are lovers run into strange capers."

It is the lady's privilege to choose the happy day, and nowadays any one of the three hundred and sixty-five may be fixed upon; but there was a time when the choice was restricted to certain seasons. An almanack for the year 1678 inserts the following notice:—

"Times prohibiting marriage:—Marriage comes in on the 13th day of January, and at Septuagesima Sunday it is out again until Low Sunday; at which time it comes in again, and goes not out until Rogation Sunday; thence it is forbidden until Trinity Sunday, from whence it is unforbidden until Advent Sunday; but then it goes out and comes not in again till the 13th day of January next following."

Although the choice of our young people is not thus curtailed, we advise them to decide if possible upon summer as the season, and the country as the place. Winter weddings and those in town are alike profoundly dispiriting. "Happy is the bride that the sun shines on," and how can we rely upon winterly rays, they are so transient and uncertain?

Then in a town, and especially in London, everything and everybody looks so much the reverse of sentimental. It seems the sole aim of the officials to get the whole affair over with as much speed as possible. The crowd which collect around the church have no interest in the bride beyond her dress. They only gather out of idle curiosity. And then in a town where are the flowers to strew the bride's path? We heard of this once being attempted in London; but, said the relater, "the camellias and azaleas had a palpable florist look about them, not in the least like those grown in a country greenhouse. They were cut with an economy of stalk and leaf which spoke plainly of a professional knife."

But we must not wander. The day being fixed, the lady has now to take into serious consideration how many bridesmaids she will have, and who they must be; while her lover—lucky man—has no such weight on his mind. Whatever the number of attendants on his bride, he only requires one to support himself, and that one is either a brother or his own most intimate friend, who for the nonce is called "the best man."

The number of bridesmaids varies from two to twelve. Six or eight are the favourite numbers, but much depends upon how many near relatives, sisters, or cousins, the bride and her groom happen to have. The selection is made from the two families as a rule, and the chief bridesmaid is the bride's sister, if she have one.

We have elsewhere spoken of the dresses to be worn by the bridesmaids on these occasions, so now we will only speak in passing as to with whom the choice should rest. This is a much-vexed question, and often causes serious dissatisfaction—not perhaps openly expressed, but inwardly felt. The bride has her ideas on the subject of material and colour and style, and it is only right that her wishes should be mainly consulted; but let her consider others as well as herself. If she does not present the costumes, she should be careful not to demand expensive ones, which will drain her friends' purses somewhat too much. Girls are often very thoughtless in this respect, and insist upon very handsome and expensive dresses, which are frequently of no use after the day for which they were ordered. And then as to colour, some colours are particularly unbecoming to one person, others to another. Endeavour, therefore, to arrange a colour and style of dress such as will suit the majority.

Often when there are a number of bridesmaids, half the number are attired in one colour, half in another. Sometimes the choice rests with the chief "maid"; but we think all should have a voice in the matter, and that they all should consider and try to fall in with the wishes of the bride-elect.

But while his *fiancée* is arranging her maids and their dresses, the bridegroom must not be idle. There are various duties devolving upon himself which demand his attention, first and foremost the arrangements for the ecclesiastical part of the ceremony.

There are four ways by which to get married in England. The first is by special licence, which enables you to be married at any time and at any place, but is not often made use of, being a very expensive method. The cost of such a licence is fifty pounds, and it is only obtainable through an archbishop.

Then there is an ordinary licence, which can be procured either at Doctors' Commons or through a clergyman (the most ordinary way), who, however, must be a surrogate, and also resident in the diocese in which the marriage is to take place. It also necessitates a personal interview between one of the parties and the clergyman, as he or she must swear that both are of age; or if minors, that they have the consent of their parents or guardians. As the marriage takes place in the parish in which the lady resides, it sometimes happens that she is obliged to apply for the licence, if the gentleman lives at a distance and finds it impossible to take two journeys, one to procure a licence and one to procure a wife. A fair friend of mine was once placed in this awkward predicament of having to procure her own licence. One of the parties must have resided during at least fifteen days in the parish in which the wedding is to take place. The fee for a licence is £2 13s. 6d., including 10s. for stamp. The licence may be used any time during the three months following the date of issue.

To be married by banns is considered to be the most orthodox way of proceeding, as well as the most economical. Banns must be published in the church of the parish in which the lady lives, and also in that in which the gentleman resides, for three continuous Sundays prior to the marriage; and the banns hold good for the three months following. The parties must have resided fifteen days previously in the parish.

Or the knot may be tied at a licensed chapel, or at the office of the Superintendent Registrar. In either of these cases it is requisite to give notice at the said office of the intended marriage, three weeks previous to the ceremony, and to obtain a certificate to the effect that this has been done, for both of which forms the modest sum of one shilling is charged. Should the marriage be by licence, the notice need not be given so long beforehand, for the marriage may be solemnised after the expiration of one whole day next after the day of the entry of the notice. For instance, if notice was given on a Tuesday, the marriage might take place on the Thursday following. The presence of the Registrar is required, both at the chapel and at the office, in which latter place a short ceremony is gone through before the Superintendent Registrar (who receives nothing for his trouble), which ceremony legalises marriages contracted in this manner.

The clergymen asked to officiate are, generally speaking, the relatives or old family friends of the bride-elect; but it is etiquette to invite the clergyman of the church in which the ceremony is to take place also to assist, and the rule is that he should in any case receive the fee, even if he be not present on the occasion, and also that he should receive an invitation to the breakfast.

"People in England," writes a French lady, "have no notion of what trouble it is to get married in France"—especially if one of the pair be a foreigner. A certificate of baptism is required, together with that of the father and mother's marriage; that of burial, too, if dead; and a written consent of grandfather and grandmother, if the latter are alive and the parents dead. The names of the parties are then put up on the door of the *Mairie* for eleven days.

To return, the bridegroom has to buy the ring, that plain gold circlet which is to remain a pledge of an indissoluble union. This should be thick, made of fine gold, and of good workmanship, fitted to endure constant, every-day wear, for the wedding ring should *never* be drawn off the finger after it has been placed there on the wedding day. It is usual to present the bride with some handsome piece of jewellery, such as a necklet or brooch, which she wears for the first time on her bridal day. The bridesmaids also generally receive a gift from the bridegroom, lockets, fans, or rings, and these are all alike given as remembrances of the day and in acknowledgment of their services. The bridegroom presents the bride and her maids with their bouquets. Such are the onerous duties of the gentleman.

And now as to the guests to be invited. The circle of acquaintance is ever widening, but a line must be drawn which will shut out many. A custom has arisen for the parents of the bride-elect to invite all friends, who are not asked as guests, to witness the ceremony. [*See page* 59.] Everybody is glad to "haste to a wedding," but only relations and one or two old friends should be invited to the actual festivity. The father and mother of the bridegroom ought to be treated as the chief guests throughout, and special attention should be paid to all the members of his family. They should stay in the house, as also should the bridesmaids.

The whirl and bustle of the day, or we might say days, before a wedding is not equalled on any other occasion. Everybody is in such a state of excitement that an uninitiated spectator might imagine that the whole household, and not one member merely, was going to be married. Apart from the arrangement of the room in which the refection is to be, the trying-on of dresses, and the packing of the bride-elect's robes, there are the presents to distract the attention, and these have to be arranged for exhibition. It is now customary for the bride's mother to issue cards for an "At Home" on the afternoon previous to the wedding day, that friends and acquaintances who are not invited to the morrow's ceremony may see the presents and bid good-bye to the bride.

The guests who have been invited to stay in the house arrive some time during the previous day. The bridegroom and his "best man" also make their appearance, but are only guests for the evening, as it is not customary for them to remain in the house of the bride's father the night before the wedding. There is usually a dinner-party, and sometimes this evening is chosen for the signing of the marriage settlements. With what anxiety is the weather watched—that great adjunct or drawback to every festivity! Well, whether fog, rain, thunder, or sunshine prevail, the ceremony must take place, and within a circumscribed time too. People creep as near to the end of this prescribed time as they possibly can, until sometimes it is quite painful as well as exciting to witness the race between parson and clock. The law is very strict on this question of time, and severe indeed is the punishment if its bounds are overstepped. Hear its stern order to the officiating priest—"The rite of marriage is to be performed between the prescribed hours, upon pain of suspension and felony with fourteen years' transportation."

Until a recent date the hours apportioned for the celebration of the rite of marriage were from eight a.m. to the hour of noon. A welcome extension of time has lately been granted, and now the ceremony may take place at any time between eight a.m. and three p.m. These added hours have altered the home arrangements in some respects. The breakfast banquet is being gradually banished, and its place is often taken by an elaborate afternoon tea at four o'clock. Half-past two o'clock is now the fashionable hour for weddings to take place.

The bride usually breakfasts in her own room, and meets the bridegroom for the first time that day at the altar, where he, with his "best man," should be waiting to receive her. All *contretemps* on these occasions are particularly awkward and uncomfortable, so we would impress the duty of punctuality on every one concerned. The guests drive first to the church, and take their seats in the chancel. The bridesmaids follow, and take up their position at the church door. The bridegroom is meanwhile waiting at the altar, supported by the "best man." A murmur and hum heard outside tell that the principal personage of the day is coming. The bridesmaids form an avenue; the bride, leaning on the arm of her father or guardian, passes through, the bridesmaids close in, and the procession moves up the aisle. The bride stands on the left hand of the bridegroom, with her chief maid of honour near her, ready to take bouquet and gloves when the time arrives for putting on the ring.

Our newly-wedded grandmothers were heartily kissed, as soon as the service was concluded, by their husband and relatives, new and old. Our mothers were more prudish, and waited for the seclusion of the vestry before offering their fair cheeks; their daughters have abolished the ceremony altogether. Our grandfathers were adorned with huge rosettes which they called "true-love knots," made of various coloured ribbons, carnation and white, gold and silver; these they wore on their hats, both on their nuptial day and for several weeks after. Our fathers wore smaller ones of white pinned on the breast of their coats, which they called "favours." Their sons do not exhibit these decorations, which only appear on servants in these days.

Altogether, not so much stir is now made at a wedding. Even the sending of cards to friends has been abandoned.

In the country, a bride's first appearance in a church is taken as a sign that she is "At Home." The old custom of offering wine to visitors on the occasion of their first call upon the bride is now no longer observed in either town or country. Small pieces of bridecake and tea are offered.

At the conclusion of the service the bride and bridegroom proceed first to the vestry, where the register has to be filled in by the clergyman, and signed by the newly-married pair, together with two or three witnesses, the principal bridesmaid and "best man" being generally the attesting parties; upon the latter also devolves the duty of distributing the fees.

The ceremonial of the Church of England has alone been selected as an example, and though there are other ways of performing this rite used by other denominations, the social usages are in all cases the same. The happy couple leave the church first, followed soon after by the bride's mother, in order that she may be at home to receive the guests, who return in the order in which they went. As they arrive they are ushered into the drawing-room, when they shake hands with the bride and bridegroom, and offer them their congratulations, and then generally turn their attention to the presents, which should be exhibited on tables set apart for this special use. The formal repast, or informal tea, whichever may have been decided upon, takes place about half an hour after the return from church.

In these modern times the bride sometimes does not appear at the formal banquet. Such retirement on her part always causes disappointment to the guests. If she is present, the newly-married pair sit side by side. If the table be a long one, they are placed on one side; if of the horseshoe shape, which is considerably the best, they are at the apex. The mother of the bride occupies the seat on the bridegroom's right hand, the father of the bride that on her left hand. The bridesmaids are seated immediately opposite. The tedious custom of proposing a series of toasts at a wedding breakfast has been suppressed by the common-sense of modern times; and even the breakfast itself now often is superseded by afternoon tea and light refreshments, especially when the wedding takes place at the fashionable and commodious hour of half-past two in the afternoon. It is the bride's duty to cut the cake. Of course an incision should previously be made. A knife is handed to her, which she puts in the cleft, and succeeds in getting a slice on to a plate. This is cut into small pieces and handed round, and everybody is expected to partake.

At the conclusion of the repast the bride retires to her room to change her dress and don her travelling costume. The hour of departure is always a trying one. Charles Lamb, in describing a wedding, says :—" I trembled for the hour which at length approached, when, after a protracted breakfast of three hours—if stores of cold fowls, tongues, botargoes, fruits, wines, and cordials can deserve so meagre an appellation—the coach was announced which was to carry off the bride and bridegroom. The chief performers in the morning pageant vanished, we idly bent our eyes upon one another. No one knew whether to take their leave or stay." No mention is here made of throwing old shoes, though it is a custom which has been long established, and one which royalty does not disdain to use at the present day. It is said to have been a symbol of renunciation, on the part of the bride's father, of all authority and dominion over her. Now it is merely regarded as wishing good luck, and a vent for the feelings consequent on separation ; as is also rice, which is now frequently showered in great profusion over the couple. Those guests who are not staying in the house, or who are not, strictly speaking, part of the wedding party, should take their leave directly after the departure of the happy couple. It is rather a tax upon the entertainers to provide amusements and keep the spirits of the party from flagging throughout this long, long day. The wisest thing to do is to send all the young people for a drive. Lawn-tennis is rather a fatiguing pastime after a wedding, and it keeps the guests without change of scene all day ; nevertheless there are enthusiasts who prefer a game of this description to the more passive pleasure of a drive. It is well on these occasions to keep all the young people together as much as possible. The elder ones are glad to rest in their rooms, or discuss the events of the day among themselves in desultory chit-chat, and thus spend the hours until dinner, at which all the visitors collect again.

Later in the evening a ball or evening party is often given in honour of the event, and to this entertainment as many people should be invited as possible, if it is to pass off with *éclat*; for, from our experience, those who have been in a state of excitement during so many hours cannot keep up their spirits and those of their home guests unless they have the help of a fresh and merry company.

CHAPTER VIII.

HOUSEHOLD APPOINTMENTS.

Immense Number and Variety of Household Appointments—A Good Manager—Styles proper for the different Rooms, Breakfast, Dining, and Drawing Rooms—Against "Best Rooms"—Temperature of Rooms—Laying the Table—List of Requisites for Entertaining Twelve People.

> "I often wish'd that I had clear
> For life six hundred pounds a year,
> A handsome house to lodge a friend,
> A river at my garden's end." — *Swift.*

THE above desire will be regarded as a particularly modest one in these ambitious days. When a similar wish is breathed in this nineteenth century, we fear that the word "thousands" stands sometimes where "hundreds" does in the original.

With the rapid strides of civilisation and refinement comes the love of luxury and the desire for means to gratify it. Then, too, temptations abound on every side. Invention has multiplied to a wonderful extent all the supposed requirements of a household, and art has adorned with grace and elegance all the commonplace routine of life. To furnish a house, what a task—what a pleasant as well as bewildering task, bewildering because of the great variety offered for choice.

What a number of things are now considered absolutely requisite that were undreamt of a few years ago! All the "appointments" add materially to the cares of the housekeeper, and though we are told that to the ladies of the seventeenth century the superintendence of their household was a labour of great extent and responsibility, owing to the ostentatious display made at the frequent banquets, still we say the task of one's housekeeper in the present day is no light one. The varied minutiæ which encumber every department require the attention of the mistress, however good and well trained her servants may be, unless she can afford to have a housekeeper. In a properly-conducted household the machinery will be well looked after, and always work out of sight, and this applies to households of every size. It is quite a mistake to suppose that a large staff of servants is necessary for comfort and perfect service. In a small house it often happens that the servants only get in one another's way. The whole matter lies in the proper management of the forces under command. "Order and method are gifts, as beauty and genius are. No two things differ more than hurry and dispatch. Hurry is the sign of a weak mind, and dispatch that of a strong one." * A good manager will never make an ostentatious display of her duties.

Though not required, as her great-grandmothers were, to attend to the culinary department in person, the lady of the house will, from her own stock of knowledge, detect "the why and the wherefore" of any little mischance or failure committed by cook, housemaid, or footman. This fault

* Colton.

or error will not be corrected or spoken of in company, but afterwards, when no one is by, the mistress will speak of what has gone wrong.

If she presides over a large establishment, she will sanction no great parade of wealth; if over a small one, let her remember that to manage a little well is a great merit. "He is a good wagoner that can turn in a little room."

It is not my intention to specify the particulars of the furniture of each room, but simply to say what their general appearance should be. Each apartment should present a distinctive feature, and that of course a comfortable and pleasing one—in fact, a house should be so furnished that each room in which we sit should in turn appear to us to be, for the time being, the pleasantest room in the place. The interior should match the exterior in style and character. Massive old-fashioned furniture, however costly, will never look well in a modern villa. Neither will new-fashioned appointments look so well in an old house; but this last is not so much to be avoided as the former. Taste, we are told, is

" ———— a discerning sense
Of decent and sublime, with quick disgust
From things deformed or disarranged." *Akenside.*

The morning-room should be cheerful and sunshiny, and wear a domestic, cosy look. It is not fitted up with any particular style of furniture. The curtains and covers will be of some kind of small-patterned chintz or cretonne, with a carpet to match. Nothing very grand or very new should find its way into this apartment—nothing stiff or formal. Tables here and there, and chairs of different sorts and sizes, a stand with plants, a small piano, a low book-case—these are the principal features in a room of this description, a general tidy *déshabille* pervading the whole.

The fittings and furniture of the dining-room must be quiet and substantial, but not too elaborate. The most prominent feature is the sideboard. The dining-table used to rank high in beauty and finish, but now that is little cared for; and, provided the top be a broad one, it may be of white or any kind of wood, in these degenerate days when the cloth is never removed for dessert.

The carpet and drapery of this room should be dark, yet warm and bright-looking, and there must be no crowd of ornaments save pictures, either oil paintings or engravings—"a room hung with pictures is a room hung with thoughts."

The library presents generally a sombre aspect; its walls are lined with lofty book-shelves, and two or three tables for the purposes of holding writing materials, pamphlets, and papers, are put in convenient positions.

And now we enter the room which, though most persons try their best, so few succeed in furnishing and arranging tastefully; for, after all, the arrangement of the furniture adds greatly to or takes away from the appearance of a drawing-room. This is, *par excellence*, the lady's room—unless the house is large enough to afford her a boudoir—and the character of the lady herself may be told by inspecting that one room. How very seldom we see the model drawing-room! No upholsterer's routine work should be visible here in stiff suites of furniture (except in case of a drawing-room reserved for special occasions); elegant refinement should reign predominant, cheerfulness should go hand in hand with taste. Easy chairs are here a *sine quâ non*. There seems to be a natural affinity between civilised beings and easy chairs, for everybody secures one where possible; therefore let them predominate in the drawing-room—some with high backs and some with low, some with straight backs and some with round, in all nooks and corners. Tables must be placed here, there, and everywhere, and yet not seem in the way; flowers or plants in vases, scattered about; and a variety of ornaments, simple or costly, as the case may be, but not too great a crowd. But the drawing-room will not be complete, nor yet have its properly comfortable look about it, unless there are plenty of books to be found on the tables, and these should be readable and entertaining volumes of prose and poetry, illustrated works, and magazines, which will not only serve their original purpose, but also supply subjects for conversation at all times, and more especially during that *mauvais quart d'heure* which precedes a dinner.

The greatest charm in such a room is, that it impresses you with the feeling that it is a resort constantly occupied, used, and enjoyed by the lady of the house. There is something indefinable, which chills and depresses one, on entering a room only used on very state occasions—a room that is just inhabited while receiving visitors; a room where the fire-irons are arranged in stiff angles; where every appliance is in formal array, and evidently never exercised in daily wear; where the tables are geometrically studded with smartly-bound unread volumes, and the prim couch and stiff chairs look as if they were meant for anything but to be sat upon.

Family comfort and enjoyment lie dead in a room of this description. This idea, once so prevalent, of having a "best room" is less general nowadays. It is a piece of folly and bad taste which has often been decried. A writer to the *Connoisseur* complains: "I have elegant apartments, but am afraid to enter them. All the furniture, except when we have company, is done up in paper; it is so genteel that we of the household must not use it commonly, which I consider a ridiculous absurdity and a great hardship."

To ensure comfort in this and all rooms, care should be taken that they are equably heated, neither too hot nor too cold—so that one is not roasted by the fire on one side and frozen by a cold draught of air on the other. Francis, sometime Emperor of Austria, said that it required as much talent to warm a room as to govern a kingdom. Of course part of that talent must be supplied by the architect; but judicious management is also required to preserve the equability; and a room full of people will become irrevocably depressed and glum when they are half-stifled with heat or shivering with cold.

In commencing housekeeping, novices are often in a difficulty how to ascertain the number of things requisite—the amount of silver, glass, and china necessary for dinner-parties, for instance. I therefore append a list, supposing twelve to be the greatest number of guests invited; of course it is easy to calculate how many more sets would be required should the number of guests be increased, or to leave out many articles, such as ice-plates and spoons, &c., which might be considered superfluities in some households. Before writing down the list, I must impress on young housekeepers the fact—and it is one that needs remembering—that, however costly and varied the viands, no dinner-table will *ever* look well unless neatness and refinement are displayed in the minor details. Very much depends on there being a fine white linen damask cloth, without crease or crumple, placed very exactly on the table. You cannot be too formal or too prim in laying out a table. The glass must be cut (not clumsy moulded glass), without fleck or flaw, bright and clear; the silver clean and polished to its utmost extent; and a clever waiter or neat-handed waitress. Neat and tidy servants are essential to the credit of a household; dirty and slovenly attendants stamp it with vulgarity. "The black battle-stain on a soldier's face is not vulgar, but the dirty face of a housemaid is," says Ruskin.

LIST OF TABLE FURNITURE NECESSARY FOR ENTERTAINING A PARTY OF TWELVE.

Four dozen forks (the medium size is now used), one dozen table spoons, three dozen dessert, one dozen teaspoons, two gravy spoons, six sauce ladles, one dozen fish knives and forks, eight or twelve salts and spoons, eighteen dessert knives and forks, soup ladle, fish slice, asparagus tongs, twelve ice spoons, grape scissors, six gilt spoons for dessert dishes.

Glass.—Two dozen tumblers, one dozen port glasses, two dozen sherry, one dozen hock, two dozen claret, one dozen champagne, one dozen finger-glasses, one dozen ice plates, glass jug and two goblets, six carafes with tumblers to match, four decanters, claret-jug, ice-pail and tongs, eighteen dessert plates and six dishes.

Table Linen.—Twelve table-cloths (six ordinary size and six larger), six long slips and six short ones for sides and ends of table, two dozen dinner napkins to match dinner cloths in pattern, six long narrow cloths for sideboard, six breakfast cloths, one dozen breakfast napkins, one dozen fish napkins, one dozen napkins for pastry and cheese, and two dozen d'oyleys.

CHAPTER IX.

BREAKFASTS.

Eating and Drinking—Breakfasts in particular—Breakfasts in the Olden Time—Breakfasts of the Present Day—How to set the Table, and what to put on it—Wedding Breakfast—Hunt and Sportsmen's Breakfast—Breakfast Dishes for the Different Seasons.

> "And then to breakfast with
> What appetite you have."
> *"Richard III."*

EATING and drinking are, as we well know, an absolute necessity if we desire to keep life within us and these crazy frames of ours together. We are told repeatedly to "eat to live, and not live to eat"—an excellent precept, and one which we should do well to keep in mind if we wish for length of days. It has been calculated that, presuming a man has four meals a day regularly, he partakes during the year of 1,460 repasts; and that if he lives to the age of sixty-five years he will have consumed a flock of 350 sheep, and those for dinner alone, and above thirty tons of liquids and solids. An alarming computation truly; but fuel must be supplied if the machinery is to be kept going. "*Venter præcepta non audit: poscit: appellat. Non est tamen molestus creditor: parvo dimittitur, si modo das illi quod debes, non quod potes,*" says Seneca (The stomach listens to no precepts: it begs and clamours. And yet it is not an obdurate creditor; it is dismissed with a small payment, if only you give it what you *owe*, and not as much as you *can*).

This chapter will be devoted to the subject of breakfasts alone; the other meals will be treated each in their order.

Breakfast is always a pleasant meal, both in winter and summer, spring and autumn; each season brings its particular enjoyment. Who will not join with the writer who says "that there is a delightful mixture of the lively and the snug in coming into one's breakfast-room of a cold morning and seeing everything prepared for us—a blazing grate (one of the first requisites for enjoyment at that period of the day and season is a good fire), a clean table-cloth and tea-things, together with tempting viands spread thereon? And if we be alone, is it not certainly a delicious thing to resume an entertaining book at a particularly interesting passage, with a hot cup of tea at one's elbow, and a piece of buttered toast in one's hand? The first look at the page, accompanied by a co-existent bite of the toast, comes under the head of intensities," says this enthusiast. And then in summer to enter a sunny, cheerful room (a breakfast-room should, if possible, be so situated as to catch the early rays of the sun), with its wide-open window, through which enters the cool, fresh morning air, the scent of flowers and the song of the birds; the table prettily decked with buds and blossoms; luscious, tempting fruit lying *perdu* in nests of green leaves; crisp rolls and golden butter, together with the more substantial dishes, which look quite able to stand a vigorous attack ! How cosy, and nice, and enjoyable all this is ! and then added to these external sources of pleasure there is that most powerful spring of happiness of all, the innate sense of freshness and vigour which most people feel at that hour of the day, when a night's rest has refreshed tired bodies and soothed weary minds. Yes, whether we join the gathering round our table one of many, or sit down to it a solitary bachelor or a secluded old maid, the breakfast hour is a pleasant one. Sydney Smith liked breakfast parties, because, he said, no one was conceited before one o'clock in the day. But in these modern times the hours creep on later and later, and a meal at four p.m. is called a "breakfast." We trust that those who partake have in reality broken their fast at a much earlier hour, and that the term is merely a misnomer.

"As soon as Phœbus' rays inspect us,
First, sir, I read, and then to breakfast."

That was the old custom, and there is a description in an old book of two noblemen who, says the chronicler, "rose with the sun, as was the custom; and after they had washed, dressed, and prayed, an attendant placed before them a very large pasty, upon a white napkin, and brought them wine, then said to them in faire words, like a man of sense : 'Sirs, you shall eat if it please you, for eating early in the morning brings great health.'" Quite a primitive mode of breakfasting, but what was then usual. The viands and beverages placed on the tables of our ancestors came under the designation of "plain plenty"; no luxuries, no variety of dishes appeared on their boards, and the following is a fair sample of an ordinary breakfast : " My lord has on his table at seven o'clock " (notice the hour is creeping nearer to noon) "a quart of beer and wine, two pieces of salt fish, six red herrings and four white ones, and on flesh days half a chine of beef or mutton boiled." Beef and brawn, herrings and sprats, seem to have been the staple dishes ; and doubtless these heavy meals were very hastily dispatched by the good old English gentlemen. They had no letters to read, no newspapers to beguile them. Booted and spurred, equipped for the chase, they quaffed their cups of malmsey or beer, cut their hunches of bread and meat in the manner of the modern ploughboy, and, having eaten heartily and hastily, would ride away for the day through wood and field, or over down and fell. The fragant odour of coffee had not been inhaled by them, and they were total strangers to the great beverage of our time—tea ; for not until the close of the seventeenth century did the berry from Mocha and the leaves from China make their appearance on English breakfast tables ; and the circumstance of a young man at Oxford drinking coffee is recorded as one worthy of remembrance.

But enough now of the days that are past. Let us turn to those which are before us ; and at the risk of being deemed partial, I must say that our breakfast tables are more inviting and present a more elegant appearance than did those of our more barbarous, if more chivalrous, ancestors. Delicate and refined habits of eating have replaced the coarse feeding of the Middle Ages.

The breakfast table is very commonly a round one, but if the dining room is used, as is often the case when there is a large party of guests, the mistress of the house often occupies the seat at table taken by the master at dinner. Before her are the tea and coffee equipage; the cups and saucers close at hand; next, the tea and coffee pots, sugar basin, cream jug, &c. In the centre of the table there should be a vase of flowers; in summer a china bowl of freshly-gathered roses, or a bunch of wild flowers, is a pretty ornament; later in the year a deep plate filled with moss, and studded with asters, dahlias, or chrysanthemums, has a good effect; at other seasons a fresh green fern—anything which adds brightness and grace to the table, but at the same time is not stiff and formal. The arrangement of flowers for a breakfast table should never be so studied or formal as that for a dinner table, nor even as the drawing-room bouquets. They should possess the distinctive feature of elegant negligence and simplicity. Fruits flank the flowers, and are placed on dishes which match the tea service. Then the various eatables—such as eggs, potted meats, fish, &c.—are placed up and down the table, and are interspersed with racks of dry toast, hot rolls, tea-cakes, and muffins, small loaves of brown and white bread, and dainty pats of butter within the reach of every one. The more substantial dishes—such as hams, tongues, and pies—are usually placed on a white cloth on the sideboard; and at an ordinary breakfast the gentlemen help themselves and the ladies also. Fish is placed upon the table, and so are the hot dishes, such as kidneys, mushrooms, or fried bacon. Before each person is set a china plate like the breakfast service, *on* which is placed a napkin and a knife and fork beside it. This plate is used for butter, bread, or toast. The plates for the meats are placed in small piles before each dish on the sideboard, so that at breakfast two plates are used at the same time; the smaller one is kept, the other changed with each course. In France the *déjeûner* used to be commenced with an egg. A boiled egg was placed before everybody, and everybody ate a boiled egg. Then the vegetables are handed—asparagus—delicious sauce as an accompaniment, or *pommes de terre frites*. After this hot fish, then meats, lastly fruits. The cups and saucers are placed beside each person, and not in formal array in front of the lady presiding, and the teapot is passed round together with the sugar and cream. There is one thing we may learn with advantage from the French mode of serving breakfast, and that is their liberal supply of plates. They are not, as a rule, noted for being "nice" in their ways, but they are worthy of imitation in this particular respect by the good people at home, who are generally inclined to be stingy and careful with the supply of plates. Even in households where "Marie" is the sole domestic, and has to fetch the water from the well, and clatter in her wooden shoes from room to room of the large château, performing her multifarious duties, she is never excused nor does she try to evade the law of clean plates. If one thing has touched an *assiette*, another must not be put upon it, so that, with the many courses at each meal, the afterwork which devolves upon Marie would overwhelm with dismay an ordinary English kitchenmaid. Appended are a series of dishes suitable for the different seasons of the year.

What has been said hitherto applies to ordinary breakfasts. Wedding breakfasts, *déjeûners à la fourchette*, are conducted in rather a different manner. They are of a more formal character than those we have been describing, and have all the form and ceremony of a dinner, both as regards waiting and table decorations. As to the viands and beverages, they are most varied, and are a curious combination of all the four meals. Soup is handed, tea and coffee, claret and champagne—everything on the table is cold, and all the dishes are very much garnished and ornamented. The table itself is set as for a dinner, in a formal, precise manner; rolls of bread in the napkins; the knives and forks on either side; all the arrangements carried out in the strictest way. Flowers and fruits are arranged either in large groups or scattered about in tiny bouquets and clusters, according to the prevailing fashion. The chief centre is occupied by the bride-cake (when the breakfast is to celebrate a wedding), which is always an imposing structure, and considered to be *the* ornament of the feast. A collation of this description should consist of cold game and poultry, hams, tongues, game pies, savoury jellies, potted meats, and fish; lobster salads, creams, jellies, custards, candied fruits, ornamental cakes, ices, &c. No trenchers of bread, no homely tea-cakes or pats of butter are seen at this kind of breakfast. The *tout ensemble* should present as glittering a display as possible. Silver, glass, and china should create a universal sparkle and glitter. It should be—

> "A table richly spread in regal mode,
> With dishes piled, and meats of noblest sort
> And savour."

The hunt breakfast and sportsmen's breakfast differ from either of those mentioned before. The table is not decorated or ornamented ; all the space is reserved for the dishes, which on these occasions make the table groan, as people say. The Lancashire motto should be adopted : " Plenty to look at, plenty to eat, and plenty to leave." No sweets are placed on the table, only substantial food, which is likely to fit those who partake for the labour and toil of the day they are commencing. Game pie is a standard dish on these occasions, cold beef, devilled turkey, broiled ham, French pies, &c. Cherry brandy is at hand for those who choose that as their beverage, and tankards of beer ; but huntsmen nowadays, as a rule, take tea and coffee.

SPRING.

Broiled trout.	Ox-palates.
Codfish cakes.	Marmalade.
Curried eggs.	Water-cresses.
Savoury omelette.	
Potted char.	Pigeon pie.
Potted beef.	Ham.
Stewed kidneys.	Spiced beef.
Pommes de terre frites.	

SUMMER.

Broiled mackerel.	Devilled chicken.
Fried soles.	Pigeons in jelly.
Broiled whiting.	Strawberries and raspberries.
Buttered eggs.	
Broiled ham.	Veal-cake.
Potted salmon.	Tongue.
Potted shrimps.	Beefsteak pie.

AUTUMN.

Broiled fresh herrings.	Fresh shrimps.
Collared eels.	Grapes.
Poached eggs.	
Potted hare.	Grouse pie.
Potted lobster.	Cold roast fowl.
Toasted mushrooms.	Ham.
Broiled pheasant.	Rolled beef.
Reindeer-tongue.	

WINTER.

Kippered haddock.	Prawns.
Bloaters.	Stewed ox-tails.
Anchovy toast.	Marmalade.
Sausages.	
Broiled mutton chop.	Melton pie.
Devilled turkey.	Brawn.
Pommes de terre frites.	Round of beef.

CHAPTER X.

LUNCHEONS.

Luncheon—Manners at Table—What to place there, and how to place it—Hot Luncheons—Cold Luncheons.

> "When hungry thou stoodst staring like an oaf,
> I sliced the luncheon from the barley loaf."
> — *Gay.*

LUNCHEON has been defined as an insult to one's breakfast and an outrage to one's dinner. It is clearly an interpolation of no very ancient date. Three meals a day—breakfast, dinner, and supper—were formerly considered as amply sufficient; but now two more have added themselves to the list, and shouldered out to a great extent the old-fashioned after-dinner tea and supper. Luncheon is one of these extra "feeds" which has squeezed itself firmly in, and now the half-hour devoted to this meal is considered indispensable. We leave it to the decision of the medical community whether long abstinence or the too frequent supplying of the inner man is the most deleterious to health. Luncheons are fairly established in most households. Sometimes they answer the purpose of dinner, and then they require to be more substantial, but still should only exhibit "an elegant sufficiency."

There should be an absence of all formality about an ordinary luncheon. Precedence is not observed; neither do the gentlemen take in the ladies. The lady of the house leads the way, followed by the others, and the gentlemen come in a body after them. It is not customary for guests feminine to doff their bonnets or out-of-door garments when invited to partake of this meal; but this latitude is not permitted to the lady presiding at her own table, who must appear in indoor morning dress.

The arrangement of the table is of a formal-informal character, inasmuch as though there is not the order and precision observed as at the dinner, it yet has a style of its own, and one that does not vary. Everything is placed upon the table at the beginning, and (unless at a very large party, where confusion would be the inevitable result) persons help themselves and one another. Gentlemen wait upon the ladies. Children, if there be any, are looked upon as servitors for the occasion, and often prove deft little waiters. At larger parties the servant stays in the room to hand the first course, the vegetables and salad; then removes the meats from the table, draws the other dishes—sweets, cheese, &c.—from the centre, and then leaves the room. It is quite allowable to push on one side the plate on which you have had tart or jelly and take another before you with fruit or cheese. An elegant disorder is perfectly distinct from a vulgar confusion.

Luncheon in small families generally consists of the cold meat, game, or poultry which remains from the dinner of the previous day; but nothing should ever come to table exactly in the same form in which it has appeared before. The appearance of the luncheon table depends very much on this being duly remembered. To make the "cold remains" look well, they should be temptingly arranged and tastefully garnished. A fowl denuded of its wings looks most uncomfortable on a table; whereas, how very different is the effect if its legs are crossed one upon the other, and the ungainly ankles ornamented with parsley! The ragged and untidy object is converted into a seemly dish.

Again, a dish of veal cutlets presents a much more appetising look when they are reared against a mound of mashed potatoes, with delicate rolls of bacon lying at their feet. A salad is more presentable and refreshing when prepared and mixed in a bowl than when the huge lettuces are alone on one dish, and the cucumber stretches its long length on another, and the beetroot and hard-boiled egg which should have garnished it are the one underground and the other in its shell. The tottering wall of jelly would look infinitely more comfortable had it been broken down and its quivering pieces put into glasses; and the fruit from last night's dessert, if re-arranged on fresh leaves. All these little niceties add wonderfully to the *tout ensemble*. Flowers should grace the whole. At luncheon the bread is not placed before each person as at dinner, but the trencher with loaf is placed on the table as at breakfast—only at luncheon a few pieces are always cut beforehand, and the board is handed round by the servant.

If a hot luncheon is required, soup may be brought to table, together with fish cakes, hashed mutton, minced chicken, veal cutlets, mutton chops, roast fowls, or any entrée, and light puddings, but cold meats and sweets are generally preferred. Of these any of the following may be selected for the luncheon table: cold lamb, pigeon, pork or beefsteak pies, pressed or roasted beef, tongue, fowls (boiled or roasted), game, veal patties, potted meats, lobsters, salad, fruit tarts, light puddings, custard, stewed fruit, jelly, blancmange, cheesecakes, tartlets, sponge or plum cake, cheese, biscuits, butter, and fruits. The beverages offered should be sherry, claret, claret cup, and light beer.

CHAPTER XI.

DINNERS

"The Dinner Question"—Less Cost and more Care—The Dinner Tables of the Last Ten Centuries—Good Cookery—Good Waiters—Invitations: Whom to Invite—Dinner *en Famille* and *à la Russe*—Carving—Table Appointments and Decorations—Arrival of Guests—Going in to Dinner—The Dinner—Wines—The Dessert—Retirement of the Ladies—Coffee—Tea—Departure.

> "Now good digestion wait on appetite,
> And health on both."   "*Macbeth.*'

> "Since Eve ate apples, much depends on dinner."
> *Byron.*

THE dinner question is one which has occupied the thoughts and been the serious study of mankind for many generations. It is curious to trace the different phases through which the art of dining has passed, during the ages in which we have any account of this king of meals, from the rude and rough manner in which the Anglo-Saxon dined down to the superb banquet of the present day. We have toiled and reflected—we still ponder the question—may it not be in consequence of our anxiety to benefit ourselves and mankind in this respect that we have, as Darwin says, "made ourselves tailless and hairless, and multiplied folds to our brain?" Each generation thinks that it has made a step in advance of the previous one. The globe has been ransacked from "China to Peru" for delicacies, novelties, and varieties of comestibles and beverages. Money can now command meats, vegetables, and fruits at any and every season of the year, and every wine that can gladden the heart of man. But sumptuous viands and rare wines alone will not ensure an enjoyable dinner; and indeed their importance is greatly over-estimated by the majority of dinner-givers. Less cost and more taste, together with more care in what are erroneously considered to be minor details, is what is desirable. Do the guests feel any the better, or enjoy their entertainment any the more, for eating gold? Asparagus at a shilling a stalk, peaches ten shillings apiece, and strawberries at two guineas a basket, serve as things to be boasted of by the purchaser; but we doubt if vegetables and fruit preternaturally forced are real luxuries. Even the hundred-guinea dish of M. Soyer is a thing more to talk about than to enjoy. Good company, good waiting, and good cookery are the secrets of success; and there are secrets hidden in each one of these essentials, simple as they appear to be, which only a host and hostess here and there have the penetration to discover. Some stumble on the rock of ostentatious display; others make the mistake of inviting too large a number of guests—a thing which is perfectly intolerable at a dinner party. This host thinks only of the wine he can set before his company; that hostess of the distinguished "lions" whom she can secure to sit at her table; and so real comfort is too seldom studied. These remarks apply just as much to a dinner *en famille* as to one *à la Russe*.

Before going into further details, let us in a few words review the dinner tables of the last ten centuries. The account of a dinner in very early times must of necessity be a scanty one, in that there would in the nature of things be but little to describe. When the dinner hour arrived, boards were brought into the hall and placed upon trestles, on whose rough surface a few plates were set, by no means equal in number to the diners, each of whom cut his food with the knife which he carried about with him for hunting purposes. When the company were seated, the meats were brought from the kitchen on the spit (so we will conclude they did not know of gravies); and such were the lawless manners of the time that the joints had to be guarded in their transit from the kitchen to the hall by ushers, who with their rods beat off the "letchers" when they attempted to seize the dinner from the cooks.

The appointments of the Normans were more numerous and various. As to the quality of the food, that depends upon taste. When dinner was announced, the guests advanced into the hall, led ceremoniously by two *maîtres d'hôtel*, who showed them their places and served them with water to wash their hands. The tables were spread with cloths, and there were goblets and cups, saltcellars and spoons. The dishes were brought in by valets, led by two esquires. A "placer" took them from the valets and arranged them on the table. The meats were eaten from large slices of bread, which were then thrown into a vessel. After this course the table-cloths were changed and the sweets came in. Lastly, the dessert appeared, which consisted of cheese and fruits, and the repast was terminated by a draught of hippocras. Although the ceremony observed in the serving of the viands was so extreme, I doubt whether the culinary department would have met with our approbation. Garlic was the favourite seasoning, and flavoured indiscriminately "fish, flesh, and fowl." We select one bill of fare for the reader's consideration—

"First course: Boar's head enarmed, and bruce for pottage; beef, mutton, pestles of pork, swan, roasted rabbit, tart.

"Second course: Drope and rose for pottage; mallard, pheasant, chickens farsed and roasted, malachis baked.

"Third course: Conigs in gravy and hare in brasé, teals roasted, woodcocks, snipes, raffyolys baked, flampoyntes."

And to describe one or two of these dishes: "Bruce" consisted of portions of pig mixed with vegetables and spices. "Drope," of almonds and onions fried in "fresh grease." "Flampoyntes" were made of pork, cheese, sugar, and pepper, fried in the same tempting liquid. A Raffyoly was a sort of patty. Pork in some form or other was a very favourite dish. Now we dream as little of placing it on our tables (except they are very homely ones) as do the Jews. Charles Lamb's rhapsody on roast pig stirs few hearts now-a-days. As we read on, we find that luxuries increase and banquets become more costly. Indeed, one is recorded the *menu* of which, though arranged for a great state occasion (the installation of an archbishop), is on such a gigantic scale that it would, I think, make even the great Gunter look aghast. Space forbids us giving more than a few of the items. 400 swans, 2,000 pigs, 4,000 pigeons, 500 stags, 104 peacocks, 4,000 cold venison pasties, 1,500 hot ditto, 8 seals, 4 porpoises, 1,000 dishes of jelly, &c. &c. &c.

The confectionery of this period was very delicate and elaborate. After each course came a subtility—that is, representations in raised pastry of castles, giants, saints, ladies, and animals, upon which legends and coat armour were painted in their proper colours.

The habit of profuse and luxurious living seems to have declined during the sixteenth and seventeenth centuries. In Henry VII.'s day the tables, as a rule, were served in great confusion; no nicety or order was observed. The art of cookery degenerated, and the manners were so rough, that often when an attractive dish made its appearance the guests displayed their greediness by scrambling for its contents. It was common, too, for gentlemen to wear their hats at this meal. Pepys remarks—"Home to bed, having got a strange cold by flinging off my hat for dinner." Desserts were discontinued, so that altogether the meals of this period were the reverse of comfortable.

Once more the art of dining became a subject of study, as the chronicles of the eighteenth century testify. One after another, luxuries of various kinds were introduced. Forks became general; and crowding after that excellent invention, a host of etceteras, without which at the present day a dinner table is not considered complete; so that in this nineteenth century almost as much consideration and thought is required to lay a table for a dinner as to place and arrange an army on a field of battle.

Having now arrived at our own times, let us stay there until the end of the chapter. Good cookery, good company, and good waiting have been laid down as the three essentials for a comfortable dinner. With reference to the first, a good household book—which this does not pretend to be—will be the best guide, together with the help afforded by the list of *menus* given at the end of this section; but there are one or two points to be noticed which are strictly within our province. The first is the error which many fall into of thinking too much about the principal dishes, and paying too little attention to their accompaniments. The French say—" A delicious sauce will cause you to eat an elephant." They are fully aware of the value of these little details, which we English are too apt to count of small importance. Sauces and gravies hold a high position. Then, again, the soup is so often a failure at our dinners; and yet, being the first thing partaken of, one would think it desirable to give the guest a good impression to start with. *C'est la soupe qui fait le soldat* is a favourite proverb of our neighbours, who also excel in this branch of the culinary art.

The second point is, not to have too many dishes attached to each course. Ample choice, so as to allow for the differences of taste, is necessary, but there should be a limit. One man cannot partake of fifty different dishes at the same meal. The perpetual repetition of "No, thank you," to the continuous stream of dishes handed to you becomes wearisome, besides which it often happens that in attempting too great a variety we run the risk of many failures. A "little dinner," at which each dish of its kind is perfect, is a far greater success than a "large one" indifferently cooked and served.

And now a word about the attendants, upon whom depends so much.

Dexterity, rapidity, and, above everything else, *quietness*, added to a thorough knowledge of his duties, form the essential requisites of a good waiter. In this department, as in others, practice alone makes perfect. How, then, is it possible for a man who has been employed in quite a different capacity to acquit himself well in this position? And yet this is frequently attempted; but it is really always a mistake to do so. It is considered the "correct thing" to have only men to serve, and so some people, when they have more persons to dinner than their one indoor man-servant can wait upon, press their out-of-door men into the service; but hands that have been accustomed to handle the spade and besom, to grooming horses, and what not, have not the delicacy of touch necessary for the handling of glass and silver. The more anxious the novice is, the more awkward and noisy will he be.

This love of show to the entire exclusion of comfort is satirised by a writer of the last century—one of that band of Essayists who did their utmost to unmask the folly of those around them. It is supposed to be the lament of a husband whose wife loved ostentation, and strove to appear the mistress of a grander establishment than she in reality possessed. A lady of title had sent word to say that she intended coming to see them on a certain day, and the host thus describes what ensued. "It would," he says, "tire you to enumerate the various shifts that were made, by purchasing, borrowing, &c., to furnish out a dinner suitable for the occasion; nor was there less ado in making ourselves and our attendants fit to appear before such company. My gardener, who had been accustomed to serve in many capacities, had his head cropped, curled, and powdered for the part of butler; one of the best-looking ploughboys had a yellow cape clapped to his Sunday coat, to make him pass for a servant in livery. During the progress of the entertainment there were several embarrassments, which might appear ridiculous in description, but were matters of serious distress to us. Soup was spilled, dishes were overturned, and glasses broken by the awkwardness of our attendants, and things were not a bit mended by my wife's solicitude to correct them." Does not our own private and uncomfortable experience vouch for the truth of this description? Have we ourselves not felt on one occasion a dish of oysters *à la crème* gliding down the back of our best dress suit, and on another had our risible faculties excited and our good manners put to the test at the same time by seeing a young waiter lying prone on the floor, surrounded on all sides by rolls of bread? And have not you, my readers, had your elbows knocked, your heads bumped, by clumsy louts? Have not your ears been annoyed by the noisy clatter of plates, the jingle of glasses, and that most unpleasant sound, the rattling of knives and forks?

Therefore, we gather that no greater mistake can be made than to make up the quantum of waiters from men who are not accustomed to the work. If the party be a small one, do not disdain the help of a "neat-handed Phyllis," or else carefully limit the number of your guests in proportion to that of your in-door men-servants. One man by himself cannot wait well on more than six people. If the dinner is a state affair, then, of course, a waitress would look out of place in the room; but in the country, friends often oblige each other by the loan of their servants at these times, and in a town it is easy to hire men who are proficients in this line.

The invitations are issued in the name of the gentleman and lady, a fortnight or three weeks beforehand. They should be answered immediately, and, if accepted, the engagement should on no account be broken. This is a very strict rule with regard to dinner parties, as it will easily be seen that the non-arrival of an expected guest would cause confusion and disarrangement of plans.

The hour is generally from seven-thirty o'clock to eight-thirty—rather a change from the olden dinner hours, which were nine or ten in the morning. There is an old saying which thus defines the division of the domestic day—

"Lever à cinq, dîner à neuf;
Souper à cinq—coucher à neuf;"

which shows that we have got very far in advance of or behind our progenitors.

Whom to invite is a consideration which requires the exercise of judgment and discretion. Dinners are generally looked upon as entertainments for married people, but it is advisable to have a few young men and maidens also. Then the people whom you invite should be of the same standing in society. They need not necessarily be friends, or all of the same absolute rank; but as at a dinner people come into closer contact one with the other than at a dance or any other kind of party, those only should be invited to meet one another who move in the same class of circles.

The talking powers of your friends have also to be considered. All the quiet people must not be asked together on one occasion, and all the talkative, noisy people on another. They must be cleverly mingled together, so that they will smoothly amalgamate both as a whole, and also one with another when placed side by side round the festive board. Real talkers have been designated as those "who have fresh ideas, and plenty of warm words to clothe them in." These invaluable people are unfortunately but rarely to be met with, but we can always find one at least among our acquaintance who has that happy effrontery of speaking incessantly, even if it be sometimes ridiculously, without overpowering every one else, and who has a hearty, cheery laugh. One such person at any rate should be secured, for there are numbers of timid people who talk fluently enough if they do not hear too loudly the sound of their own voices, and thus the chatter of one talkative friend will serve as a cover, and will induce much by-conversation.

The invitations having been issued, we must turn to the arrangements of the dinner table. Dinners *à la Russe* have been in great favour during the last few years, particularly with the gentlemen, and no wonder, for then they are relieved from the responsible task of carving. When a dinner is served in this style all the meats, poultry, and game are placed on the sideboard and carved by the butler; but this plan cannot be attempted unless there happen to be a large staff of servants. Carving is not so much practised as it might be. "However trifling some things may seem, they are no longer so when about half the world thinks them otherwise. Carving, as it occurs at least once in every day, is not below our notice. We should use ourselves to carve adroitly and genteelly." So says Lord Chesterfield; but how seldom do we meet with "a good carver"! Once upon a time there were schools where this art was taught. Wooden models of various birds, joints, &c., carved out into pieces as the original ought to be, and fastened together by threads or glue, were placed before the pupils, whose business it was to separate them by blunt instruments. At one time this duty of carving was apportioned to the lady of the house, while the host dispensed the wine. Lady Wortley Montagu used to dine by herself an hour or two beforehand, in order that she might perform this office at her father's table, and she only followed the general custom of that day.

Well, whichever way the dinner is served, the appointments of the table are the same. A white cloth of the finest linen damask is spread *very* exactly on the table. Down each side and along each end may be long and short slips, which are drawn off at the conclusion of dinner and before the dessert. Before each seat is placed a napkin, folded in some intricate form, and a roll of bread lies within. A knife, fork, and spoon are ready for immediate use, and on the right hand of each person are set a sherry, claret, and champagne glass. No tumblers are seen on the table at modern dinner parties. There should be a small saltcellar within easy reach of every guest; also a water carafe and glass. The old-fashioned epergne, which used to grace the centre of the table, has retired into obscurity, and into its place have stepped plants in ornamental pots, and vases of all shapes and sizes filled with cut flowers. Every fashion has its day. One favourite is perhaps of somewhat fantastic form, but is very graceful and pretty withal. A plateau of plate-glass occupies the centre of the table. On its surface here and there are small china water-fowl or water reptiles holding or supporting bouquets of flowers. The edges of this miniature lake are closely bordered with bright-coloured flowers or green ferns, which are placed in long glass troughs. This design is very effective on a large table, but the plateau would look rather too much on a small one. A less pretentious idea is that of a long oval board, covered with crimson velvet or plush, on which are grouped, according to fancy, clusters of small glass or china vases with flowers. The effect of this is heightened if silver candlesticks are placed here and there on the board. All the table decorations now in vogue are low in form, so that the company are not hidden from one another, and yet can have their eyes refreshed by the sight of beautiful flowers; and the flowers again are not concentrated into large groups, but are scattered up and down the table, at the same time all forming part of a preconcerted plan of decoration. Flowers placed on a dinner table should be all of a choice kind. Ferns and moss are great helps in the arrangement of them. The dessert dishes take their places amidst the flowers, and should be tastefully arranged and decorated. The fruits make as tempting a display as possible. Grapes in their own green leaves, strawberries and cherries piled high on their respective dishes, peaches, apricots, and plums ensconced each in a separate leaf, so that they may not be robbed of their delicate bloom by too close contact with their fellows—pines and melons taking their stand as the chief personages. Mingled with all these fruits, sprays of ferns and the ice-plant give a cool and refreshing appearance to the dish. Crystallised fruits sparkle and glitter; the more sober walnut and filbert, disdaining decoration of any kind, as unbecoming to their respective characters, complete the general list of after-dinner delicacies. All these dishes, and as many more as you please, are placed on the table at the commencement, and if the dinner is served *à la Russe* remain the sole occupants; if otherwise, the other dishes are placed and replaced according to the courses.

No wine is put upon the dinner table.

The dinner table is ready. Let us hope that the host and hostess, and more particularly the latter, are ready too, and in their drawing-room before the hour named for the arrivals, and that the rooms are properly arranged and lighted, so that there need be no sign of hurry or confusion at the sound of the first bell. The lady should place herself in a position so as to be easily accessible to all comers, as each guest ought to pay his or her respects to her first. Punctuality should be strictly observed. In the country half an hour's latitude is allowed, and in town a quarter of an hour's grace is given; and surely everybody, if they tried, could calculate their time so that they should arrive neither too early nor too late, but hit the happy medium; then all the discomfort and awkwardness caused by waiting after the appointed hour for some late-coming guest entailed upon host, hostess, and all the assembled company, together with the especial agony suffered by the cook, would be happily and easily avoided.

This dread of non-punctuality on the part of some one constantly destroys the peace of mind of the mistress of the house as the hour approaches; and indeed a dinner party throughout is a trying ordeal to a young and unseasoned hostess.

She should, to act her part well, be familiar with every little drawing-room ceremonial—all the laws of precedence and the whole etiquette of hospitality. Whatever unfortunate *contretemps* or catastrophe may happen, her equanimity must not be in the slightest degree disturbed. She must be "mistress of herself though china fall," and she must endeavour to keep the ball of conversation ever on the move.

The host communicates to each gentleman the name of the lady he is to take in to dinner. If they are strangers to each other, the host introduces his friend to the lady. When the "guests are met and the feast is set," the butler announces the latter to his master, who then offers his arm to the lady appointed to be escorted by him. This should be either the oldest lady, the lady of the highest rank, or the greatest stranger; or if there be a bride present, the lot falls upon her. The other guests follow arm-in-arm, and the hostess closes the procession, escorted by the gentleman who has been appointed to the honourable post, and who has been elected for one of the three reasons above-mentioned, as being the oldest or of highest rank, &c. On arriving at the dining-room, the host's seat is at the bottom of the table, and his wife's at the top, unless the fashion be adopted of occupying places opposite one another in the middle of each side, which is sometimes the case when the table is a long one. The host places his lady on his right hand, and she is considered the starting-point for the waiters, who should always offer each dish first to her. The gentleman who has accompanied the hostess is seated on her right hand, and should offer to carve for her should the dishes be placed on the table for that purpose. In order to facilitate the arrangement of the rest of the company, a card is laid on the table before each seat, on which is written the name of the guest by whom it is to be appropriated. For this purpose many pretty and fantastic devices have been designed. Sometimes a plan of the table is laid in the drawing-room, so that the gentleman having studied it may be able at once to lead the lady he escorts to her seat, and thus confusion is avoided. The servant places a plate of soup before each person in order, and it is etiquette to begin immediately that it is set before you (the ladies having, however, first withdrawn their gloves), as well as to take it quickly. Of course all food should be silently masticated. No sound is more disagreeable than that of a company "feeding like horses, when you hear them feed."

At a large party no one ever thinks of partaking of the same viand twice. At a dinner *en famille*, where "you see your dinner before you," it is permissible, but never then with respect to soup and fish. Beau Brummel, speaking contemptuously of some one, said—" He is a fellow, now, that would send up his plate twice for soup."

At a formal dinner guests are not asked their choice. This is quite unnecessary, for they have their *menu*, and so can accept or reject the different dishes that are handed to them. The *entrées* and the jellies, creams, &c., are handed on electro-silver dishes, and guests help themselves. Of the other meats, small pieces are placed on plates and offered by the servants.

It will be seen by the *menus* appended what the different courses are, and in what order they come. We will now speak of the wines.

Is it needful to say that they, like everything else, should be good? Bad cookery is deleterious, but bad wines are positively poisonous; so if the host's purse will not allow him to give his guests good champagne or hock, or any of the more expensive wines, let him offer only good sherry and claret. The difficulty of procuring good wines is certainly very great. Money even will not always secure them, although it may naturally be expected to do so. The only sure way of obtaining wine at once good and genuine is to go to a merchant of undoubted respectability.

The qualities of good wine are thus quaintly described by Neckam, a writer of the twelfth century:—"Clear as the tears of a penitent, so that a man may see distinctly to the bottom of his glass; its colour should represent the greenness of a buffalo's horn. When drunk it should descend impetuously like thunder, sweet-tasted as an almond, creeping like a squirrel, leaping like a roebuck, strong like the building of a Cistercian monastery, glittering like a spark of fire, subtle as the logic of the schools of Paris, delicate as fine silk, and colder than crystal."

No wine is placed on the dinner table, and it is the province of the butler to hand the proper kind at the proper time. Sherry is offered with soup. With the fish light wines, such as hock, chablis, and sauterne. Champagne accompanies the joint. Port wine never makes its appearance now until dessert, when it divides the honours with sherry, madeira, and claret. Fifty years ago the practice of taking wine with one another was in full force. This was a very old custom. It was prevalent amongst the Greeks and the Anglo-Saxons, and the latter always accompanied the ceremony with a kiss. A writer of Henry VIII.'s day, in laying down the rules of etiquette, suggests as one of them that when any one will drink to the health of another he must fix his eye upon him for a moment and give him time, if it be possible, to swallow his morsel.

The oft-repeated phrase, "May I take wine with you?" is no longer heard at modern dinners. The formality became a troublesome one, and has gradually fallen into disuse, except at those convivial meetings at colleges, known by the name of "Wines," where youths still pledge one another in the "cup of refreshment," and have yet a peculiar little ceremony—from whom derived deponent sayeth not—that of three linking their arms one within the other, and, thus enchained, they imbibe and pass good wishes round this small circle one to the other.

One other old custom has, we are glad to say, been almost chased away, and that is the habit of pressing hospitality. There was a day when it was the mark of good-breeding "to cram a poor surfeited guest to the throat, and the most social hours were thrown away in a continual interchange of solicitations and apologies." We say "almost." Would that it were quite extinct; but here and there uncomfortable hosts and hostesses are encountered who, out of kindness, we know—but it is *most* mistaken—repeatedly invite and urge their guests to partake of this and that after they have politely declined. To say the least, this conduct is in extremely bad taste. True hospitality lies in offering freely what you have, leaving the guest at liberty to take or pass by what he pleases; not in leading him to take what you may please against his own inclination, simply to oblige you, and so to escape further importunity. This liberty extends to those who, as a matter of taste or principle, choose to abstain altogether from wine, for whom seltzer or other agreeable mineral waters should be provided.

At the conclusion of dinner, the table is cleared of everything but the dessert dishes and flower decorations. The crumbs are taken off on to a plate by means of a silver or wooden knife, and the slips, if used, are then withdrawn. A dessert-plate, on which is a d'oyley, finger-glass, and silver knife and fork, is placed before each guest, together with three wine-glasses. On very state occasions the finger-glasses (which, when used, should be small, and not contain much water) are not put on the table, but in lieu a golden or majolica bowl filled with rose-water and napkin attached is passed round on the table, or offered by a servant. The dessert dishes are brought more forward from the centre of the table, and embossed spoons placed beside the dishes. The wine is put on the table before the host, and then handed once round by the butler. The servants hand the principal dishes one after another to each guest, and then leave the room. The hostess very soon rises, looking at the same time at the lady on her husband's right hand, who with the rest of the ladies rises from her seat. The gentlemen do the same. The host, or some gentleman more conveniently near it, opens the door, and the ladies troop out and settle themselves in the drawing-room. The servant brings cups of coffee and hands them round, and takes some to the gentlemen in the dining-room. The ladies are not left very long to themselves, as it is not now the practice for gentlemen to drink much wine after dinner. They ought, therefore, soon to adjourn to the drawing-room. The servants then re-appear, one carrying a tray on which are cups of tea, the other a salver on which rest the sugar basin and cream jug. These are handed round. Sometimes music is introduced. The half-hour or so after dinner quickly flies. At half-past ten or eleven the guests begin to depart. On the arrival of each carriage, a servant announces it quietly to the owner.

As the foregoing remarks have treated somewhat exclusively of so-called "stylish" dinners, it may be as well to make some remarks on the manner in which those given with less ostentation should be conducted. Although there is not quite so much state and ceremony observed in a dinner *en famille*, yet there is by no means the same freedom and latitude allowed as at luncheons and other meals. The table is set with care and precision; the different courses are placed on it and removed in proper order; but no dish should be taken off the table until all the plates have been previously removed; neither should one be placed on the table while any belonging to the former course remains. The dishes containing vegetables and sauces should be kept on the sideboard, and are always handed. The host may offer to serve his guests a second time from the joint or poultry, but not with soup or fish. Gentlemen carve and assist their neighbours, and should notice anything that is wanting, passing salt, mustard, or pepper, if within their reach, or asking the servant to bring it; but never attempt to leave their seats to go in search of what they need, though custom allows them to do so at breakfast and luncheon.

SPRING (April, May, June)—for Six.

Soup.
Spring Soup.

Fish.
Salmon.

Entrées.
Stewed Pigeons, with Cherries.
Beef à la mode.

Removes.
Quarter of Lamb.
Spring Chickens, with Tongue.
Cucumber.

Game.
Salmi of Larks.

Sweets.
Fruit Jelly.   Soufflé.   Gâteau Napolitain.
Cheese Straws.
Cheese.   Biscuits.   Butter.

Ices.
Brown Bread Cream.   Lemon Water.

Dinners.

Spring—for Twelve.

Soup.
Asparagus.
Vermicelli.

Fish.
Salmon.   Plain Whitebait and Devilled Whitebait.

Entrées.
Beef Olives.   Quenelles of Rabbit.
Lobster Cutlets.   Reform Cutlets.

Removes.
Quarter of Lamb.   Capon, with Ham.
Green Peas.

Game.
Quails.   Plovers.

Sweets.
Iced Soufflé.
Fruit Jelly.   Pine-apple Cream.
Gooseberry Tart.
Ramakins.   Russian Salad.

Ices.
Vanilla Cream.   Orange Water.

Fruit.
Strawberries.   Cherries.   Melons.

SUMMER (July, August, September)—for Six.

Soup.
Julienne.

Fish.
Red Mullet.

Entrées.
Lobster Cutlets. Ragout of Sweetbreads.

Removes.
Haunch of Lamb.
York Ham and Green Peas.

Game.
Quail or Larks.
Grouse (August).
Partridges (September)

Sweets.
Iced Soufflé.
Strawberry Cream. Lemon Sponge.
Plovers' Eggs.
Gorgonzola Cheese. Butter.

Ices.
Pine-apple Cream. Cherry Water.

Fruit.
Pine-apples. Strawberries. Cherries. Apricots. Melons

Dinners.

Summer—for Twelve.

Soup.
Oxtail.
Bisque.

Fish.
Salmon.   Smelts.

Entrées.
Curried Eggs.   Sweetbreads and Mushrooms.
Vol au Vent à la financière.

Removes.
Iced Asparagus.

Game.

Quails.	Larks (July).
Grouse.	Black Cock (August).
Partridges.	Black Cock (Sept.).

Sweets.
Ice Pudding.
Strawberry Jelly.   Chartreuse of Apricots.
Confiture of Nectarines.   Iced Meringues.
Cheese Straws.
Cheese.   **Butter.**

Ices.
Neapolitan Cream.   Raspberry Water.

Fruit.
Pine-apples. Strawberries. Cherries. Apricots. Melo

AUTUMN (Oct., Nov., Dec.)—for Six.

Soup.
Artichoke.

Fish.
John Dory.

Entrées.
Curried Ox-palates.   Larded Sweetbreads.

Removes.
Saddle Mutton.   Guinea Fowl.
Tomatoes.

Game.
Woodcock.

Sweets.
Cabinet Pudding.
Noyau Jelly.   Charlotte Russe.
Ramakins.
Cheese.   Butter.

Ices.
Vanille Cream.   Lemon Water.

Fruit.
Pine-apple.   Pears.   Grapes.   Medlars.   Filberts.

Dinners.

Autumn—for Twelve.

Soup.
Clear Turtle.
White.

Fish.
Cod.   Sparling.

Entrées.
Mutton Cutlets, with Tomato Sauce.
Oyster Patties.   Sweetbreads.
Beef Olives.

Removes.
Haunch of Mutton.   Turkey Poult.

Game.
Pheasants.   Snipe.

Sweets.
Bakewell Pudding.
Wine Jelly.   Italian Cream.
Gateau de Pommes.   Chocolate Cream.
Fondu of Cheese.   Savoury Eggs.

Ices.
Vanilla Cream.   Currant Wine.

Fruit.
Pine-apple.   Pears.   Grapes.   Medlars.   Filberts

WINTER (Jan., Feb., March)--for Six.

Soup.
Brunoise.

Fish.
Crimped Cod.

Entrées.
Fricandeau of Veal.

Removes.
Saddle Mutton.   Pullet.
Sea Kale.

Game.
Wild Duck.

Sweets.
Apple Soufflé.
Ratafia Cream.   Lemon Sponge.
Prawns.
Roquefort Cheese.   Butter.

Ices.
Coffee Cream.   Raspberry Water.

Fruit.
Apples.   Pears.   Medlars.   Grapes.   Walnuts.

WINTER—for Twelve.

Soup.
Palestine.

Fish.
Turbot.   Whiting.

Entrées.
Fricandeau of Beef.   Stewed Pigeons.
Quenelles of Lobster.   Reform Cutlets.

Removes.
Haunch Venison.   Turkey.
New Potatoes.   Asparagus.

Game.
Teal.   Guinea Fowl.

Sweets.
Plum Pudding.
Vanilla Cream.   Meringues.
Maraschino Jelly. Confiture of Fruit.
Ramakins.
Stilton.   Butter.

Ices.
Coffee Cream.   Strawberry Water.

CHAPTER XII.

TEAS.

High Teas—What to put on the Table, and how to place it—Arrangement of Drawing-room—Five o'clock Teas.

> "—— while the bubbling and loud-hissing urn
> Throws up a steaming column, and the cups
> Which cheer but not inebriate wait on each."
> *Cowper.*

"TEA" is supposed to be essentially the ladies' meal; but there are countless numbers of the opposite sex who, while they swallow "just an odd cup because it is made," experience as much enjoyment as those for whose delectation it was said to have been brewed. There are two classes of teas —"great teas" and "little teas": the "high" or "meat" teas, which come under the first denomination, and "handed tea," or "afternoon tea," which place themselves under the latter. The first of these is quite a country institution, and scarcely known to the dwellers in towns. Now a tea, of whatever kind, may be made one of the most agreeable of meals; for tea always seems to produce sociability, cheerfulness, and vivacity. There is an air of comfort and home which hovers over the tea table, one which the more formal dinner table can never present. What more welcome and cheering sight can meet our eye on the return from a long journey or distant excursion, or from a hardly-contested battle on the lawn-tennis ground, than the hissing, steaming urn, the array of cups and saucers, the sociable, genial air which the tea table invariably presents? Let us first speak of "high teas," which, as we have remarked, are most in fashion in the country, and for this reason: late dinners interfere with the social, informal life that country people are wont to lead, and those who are on hospitable thoughts intent have not the same opportunities afforded them of carrying out their wishes. For instance, it would be impossible in many households to invite twenty people to dinner at a few days' notice; or if several friends happened to call, bringing their visitors with them, they could not be asked to stay if the evening meal were a dinner; but, in either case, it is quite feasible when tea is in question. Very pleasant gatherings may take place in this way, either in summer as a termination to archery or lawn-tennis, or in winter as a prelude to music, round games at cards, or charades.

A white cloth is always laid on the table for "high tea," and on it down the centre are placed flowers, and in summer, fruits. Nothing looks more tempting than bowls of old china filled with ripe red strawberries, and jugs of rich cream by their side. Glass dishes containing preserved fruits of different colours, such as apricots, strawberries, marmalade, &c., take their stands at short intervals. Cakes of various kinds—plum, rice, and sponge; and then within easy reach of the "tea-drinkers" are hot muffins, crumpets, toast, tea-cakes, and what not. At one end of the table the tea-tray stands, with its adjuncts; at the other the coffee is placed, also on a tray. The sideboard is the receptacle of the weightier matters, such as cold salmon, pigeon and veal and ham pies, boiled and roast fowls, tongues, ham, veal cake; and should it be a very "hungry tea," roast beef and lamb may be there for the gentlemen of the party.

The servants should be expert and handy, as there is a good deal of waiting to be done. One should hand the cups of tea on a waiter, together with sugar and cream; another should do the same with coffee, and both should take notice of the empty cups, and take them to be re-filled. Then there should be one to carve and help at the sideboard, and another to change the plates, hand bread-and-butter, &c. Very often the gentlemen wait to a great extent upon the ladies and themselves on these occasions. After the fruit has been handed, the servants leave the room. It is usual for the party to remain a short time at the table after the conclusion of the meal.

Sometimes a dance on the lawn, or on the drawing-room carpet, music, talk, or charades end an entertainment of this kind; but if dancing is not introduced, the success of a tea depends much upon the arrangement of the reception rooms.

The furniture should be so arranged that the rooms may look full, and yet progress be not impeded. Tables and chairs should be so placed that the guests naturally form themselves into little groups, and can with ease pass from one knot to another. A room stiffly arranged will destroy all the wish for conversation and mirth, and also the power of producing it as well. And, again, an immediate depression follows the fatal moment when, either through forgetfulness or ignorance, the guests form themselves into an unbroken circle round the room. Few people have the *sang froid* to talk, much less talk freely and well, when every one can hear their remarks; and yet few are too bashful to converse in a small group. It really requires that the hostess should keep her eye upon her company in order to prevent this catastrophe, and to disperse them in time, for once this circle formed, it is almost an impossibility to break it up. A gloom pervades, hilarity ceases, only an occasional remark is ventured upon, and the party is converted into a Quaker's meeting, simply from this one circumstance.

"Little teas" take place in the afternoon. Now that dinners are so late, and that "teas proper" are postponed in consequence to such an unnatural hour as ten p.m., the want is felt of the old-fashioned meal at five, and so it has been reinstated, though not in quite the same form as before. The modern afternoon tea takes place about five, and the invitation is by card, intimating that Mrs. —— will be "At home" on such an afternoon. No answer is necessary. When the day arrives, if you are disengaged, and so disposed, you call upon your friend, are ushered into her drawing-room, and there you find her and others who have come on the same errand as yourself. The tea equipage is placed on a table near to the lady of the house, who herself dispenses the tea. Usually this equipage is one specially designed for these occasions. The cups and saucers are smaller than those in use at other meals, and are of a more dainty and refined character. The other accompaniments also are on a smaller scale—the spoons, sugar basin and tongs, cream jug, are distinctively small. No plates are brought into the room except those which hold cake or rolled bread and butter. Gentlemen, of course, will tender their services; but they should not be too officious or over-anxious to do their duty. There are men who will perpetually be handing cake, and offering to do this, that, and the other about the tea-tray. People do not assemble at these five o'clock teas to eat and drink, but merely to see and talk to each other, and take a cup of tea the while as a refreshment. Small tables should be placed here and there, so that people can group round them and use them.

If these afternoon receptions are on a large scale, it is necessary for servants to hand the tea, or for the tea to be poured out by a servant in another room, to which each guest is asked to go by the lady of the house some time during the hour they remain in the house; but as "little teas" are thoroughly social gatherings, servants should be excluded if possible. Several new features have lately been introduced into this phase of social life when guests go by invitation. Enthusiasts of whist collect their forces and enjoy a good rubber between afternoon tea and dinner. A dance on the carpet finds favour with the young people. Sometimes the hostess entertains her friends by engaging a professional musician or a reciter to exhibit their talents. We do not know whether country people are so far demoralised as to introduce these entertainments, but it is, at any rate, a London fashion. You take your departure whenever you feel inclined, but should on no account stay later than seven o'clock.

CHAPTER XIII

SUPPERS.

Suppers give place to Dinners—Roman Bill of Fare—Appointments of the Table—French Display—Our Supper Tables—Impromptu Suppers—Ball Suppers.

> " Is supper ready, the house trimmed,
> Rushes strewed, cobwebs swept ?"
> *Shakespeare.*
>
> " ——— Soft he set
> A table, and threw thereon
> A cloth of woven crimson, gold, and jet.
>   Forth from the closet brought a heap
> Of candied apples, quince, and plum, and gourd,
> With jellies smoother than the creamy curd,
> And lucent syrups tinct with cinnamon,
> Manna and dates, and spiced dainties every one
> From silken Samarcand to cedared Lebanon."
> *Keats.*

THIS meal, which used to be in all countries one of the most important, has now given way to its great rival, dinner, and has itself sunk into comparative insignificance. Supper in the olden times was the second meal in the day, at which the whole household met together. It was served in the hall, with much the same form and service as dinner; the table was plentifully covered with good things, and the company began and ended their repast by washing their hands, a parting cup was then handed round, and the adjournment from the supper table was to bed. Thus the good people appear to have ignored their own adage, "After supper run a mile." If any distinguished personages were to be entertained, either at Court or elsewhere, the invitation was always to supper.

The medical fraternity give this meal a very bad name, and shake their heads at hot suppers particularly; but there are times and seasons when this meal must be included in the day's list—for instance, it is more convenient for some households to dine in the middle of the day, then the evening meal becomes a supper; or when a business man returns home late from the City, he looks forward to his cosy, well-earned supper. At an evening party or ball the supper also forms a very important element. The Romans supped at three p.m., and, amongst other equally to us uninviting viands, used then to eat ass, dog, and snails. The following bill of fare is not a very tempting one to modern palates, although an immense improvement on dog and donkey:—"Sea hedgehogs, oysters, asparagus, succeeded by venison, wild boar, and sea nettles, concluded by fowl, game, and cakes." I think we may fairly claim that our suppers—little or big—are more civilised and dainty than this.

The arrangements of the table are of the same formal and precise nature as those of a dinner, and all the appointments should shine and glitter, as good glass and honest silver always will if servants do their duty by them. Few, perhaps, even of the wealthiest, nowadays make a display equal to that of the French Court in the luxurious age of Louis XV. Such entertainments as the following were by no means extraordinary:—"The table looked like a mountain of snow; its surface was, according to the fashion, ribbed in fanciful and waving plaits, so as to represent the current of a stream crisped by a passing breeze. This stream bore upon its bosom a proud array of gold and silver vases, crystal cups and goblets, all of rarest workmanship. There were—

> 'Dishes of agate set in gold, and studded
> With emeralds, sapphires, hyacinths and rubies.'

Fancy ran riot amongst the endless varieties of piquant viands; pyramids of confectionery, piles of choicest fruits appeared at intervals, while antique-shaped urns steamed with the rich produce of the grape—for wines were then drank hot and spiced for the most part." But we must come away from fairy-land to our more sober country and every-day doings.

Supper tables can be made to look nice and tempting enough by the bestowal of a little care and ingenuity upon them. The garnishing of the dishes adds greatly to the general appearance of the table, as well as the neatness and precision with which those dishes are placed upon it. The eye may be gratified as well as the palate, but at the same time due care must be taken that all is not merely glitter and show, that appearances are not deceptive, but that our further acquaintance with what is spread before us increases our first admiration, and does not turn it into disappointment and disapprobation.

If the supper is for a small number, on an ordinary occasion, meats and sweets may be placed upon it which have appeared before, only they need not have precisely the same form. Of this we have spoken elsewhere, with regard to cold luncheons; and this applies equally to suppers; but supposing hot dishes were required with little notice, why, then the remains of the chicken might be fricasseed, what is left of the rabbit made into a curry, a savoury omelette is quickly prepared, oysters are soon scalloped and mushrooms grilled, beef can be minced, a sole fried, spinach boiled and crested with poached eggs, sweetbreads cooked, macaroni and cheese made to agree, or a partridge roasted. Any of these dishes may be quickly served, and they are all suitable for the supper table. Then as to sweets. Tarts containing any kind of fruit, and moulds of every description, together with cakes, cheese, biscuits, and butter, form the second and last course.

Now we turn to a more formidable banquet, a supper in connection with an evening party or ball, which closely resembles a wedding breakfast. Flowers and fruits should occupy the middle of the table, from one end to the other. Bonbons, crackers, and ornamented cakes should spring up on all sides, together with frothy trifles, quivering jellies, snowy creams, and light soufflés, all placed in glass dishes. Then there are oyster patties, savoury jellies, lobster salads, veal cakes, and the more substantial dishes of cold salmon, game pie, boiled turkey, fowls boiled and roasted—these should have been carved before coming to table, and tied together in their original form with white satin ribbon, so that the person before whom they are placed has no further trouble than to untie the bow and put each piece on a plate as required. Hams, tongues, and game, everything is cold at these suppers except soup, which is now often handed in cups. Neither vegetables nor cheese show themselves. Ices should be provided, and the beverages are sherry, claret, light and sparkling wines, and the different kinds of cups, champagne being the greatest favourite.

CHAPTER XIV.

BALLS.

Seasons for Balls—Dances—Different Styles—Public Balls—How to manage them—Tickets—Introductions—Duties of Stewards—Fancy Dress Balls—Private Balls—Rooms necessary—Good Dancers—Music—Lights—Decorations—Cloak-room — Tea-room — Drawing-room—Ball-room—Duties of the Entertainers to their Guests—Partners to their Partners—Card-room—"Cinderella Dances."

> "I could be pleased with any one
> Who entertained my sight with such gay shows,
> As men and women, moving here and there,
> That coursing one another in their steps,
> Have made their feet a tune."
>
> *Dryden.*

WINTER one would think to be the proper and only season for the enjoyment of the dance. When sharp north-easters blow, and icicles hang pendent from every roof and tree, then is the time for active exercise, by day and night, on the ice-bound lake and in the mazy whirl in the ball-room. But young blood always enjoys being in motion; and dancing on the green turf at the close of a summer picnic, after an afternoon's hard work on the lawn-tennis ground, or a carpet waltz begun impromptu on an autumn evening—each and all are acceptable, and enjoyed with as much zest as the Twelfth-night ball is in cold January; at no season is dancing considered unseasonable.

It is amusing to see in what lights the ball-room is viewed by the chaperons and the chaperoned. It has been described by one of the former as "a confined place in which poor creatures are condemned by fashion to hard labour;" while to one of the latter, the motion of the dancers appears to be like

> "A fine sweet earthquake gently moved
> By the soft wind of dispersing silks."

Then, again, the style of dancing is depreciated by the elderly frequenters, who say there is no such thing as dancing nowadays, it is only running round the room. "In my young days," say they, "there was a heartiness in the dancing, which it lacks now; the young people had then some mettle in their heels." When we come to inquire what this much admired and lamented style was, we find that it might thus be described in the language of Aristophanes, "He strikes and flutters like a cock; he capers in the air, he kicks up his heels to the stars." Certainly, we of the present day can lay claim to more grace and elegance, if not to equal agility.

The list of dances now in fashion is of greater length than it was some years ago. At that time the valse, the lancers, and the galop seemed to occupy the programme. The two first dances still continue to be the favourites, but others have been re-introduced: the polka takes turn with the valse, and the quadrille sometimes takes the place of that ever-bewildering, never-to-be-remembered maze, the lancers. The coquettish cotillion, the friendly country dance, and the merry reel are frequently danced: of the two latter, the Swedish dance and the Highland schottische are chiefly chosen. Even the stately minuet, the galliards, the bransle, and the torreano, danced by courtly knights and dignified dames centuries ago, are likely to be brought forward again.

First let us speak of public balls, amongst which are county balls, hunt balls, hospital balls, bachelors' balls—in fact, any ball for which tickets have to be bought in order to gain admittance. When a ball of this kind is in prospect, the first thing to do is to form a committee of gentlemen who will take an interest in such a proceeding, and devote their time and energies to carrying the plan out effectually. The first proceeding of the committee is to ask ladies of rank and position to become patronesses. When their consent is obtained, the ball should be announced in the newspapers, together with a list of the lady patronesses, and the names and addresses of the stewards. These stewards are appointed to manage the ball itself, and in order to keep the company select the tickets can be obtained through them and the lady patronesses alone. In the case of a county ball, not only must the names of those wishing to buy tickets be sent in, but if they are strangers they must present an introduction from some one personally known to the stewards or lady patronesses, as the case may be. A public hall or room is engaged for the occasion, and as a proper decorator is employed, we will not interfere with his ideas, but leave him to turn the bare and dreary room into a smiling, brilliant hall, a feat generally very satisfactorily accomplished.

At these balls introductions are effected through the stewards, who wear some badge of office in the shape of a rosette or ribbon. If a gentleman asks him to find a partner, he may go to any lady he sees who is not dancing, and say, "May I introduce you to a partner for this dance?" The steward, having performed his part, retires, and the gentleman asks the lady if he may have the pleasure of a dance with her. The steward's post is no sinecure, for his aim should be not only that a ball should go off well, as the phrase is, but that everybody should enjoy it; so if he sees any lady not dancing much, he should seek out gentlemen whom he can introduce to her as partners. Then the forming of the square dances devolves upon him; any alterations in the programme must be communicated through him to the musicians; he must see as well as he can that the chaperons have been taken in to supper; and if the spirit of the entertainment appears to be flagging, put forth all his energies to revive it. Public balls begin about eleven p.m. and end about four a.m.

Fancy dress balls are not of very frequent occurrence; but when the arrangements are carried out with spirit and ingenuity they present at once a most unique, gay, and imposing spectacle. People who attend them must go dressed in any costume except that they usually wear. Many assume well-known historical characters; others adopt the national costumes of different countries. It is always well to choose a character and style of dress suitable to the character, face, and figure of the wearer; for instance, a fair-complexioned person should not assume the garb of an Italian or a gipsy, nor a small and insignificant one appear as

Henry VIII. or Marie Antoinette. The portraits of the old masters afford ample and reliable information as to costume on a wide range for those who take part in these revelries.

The first thing to be considered before deciding to give a private ball is whether you have rooms enough, and whether they are fitted for the purpose. In order to have your arrangements complete, six or seven rooms at least should be set apart for this festivity—two cloak-rooms, tea and refreshment room, drawing-room for the reception, ball-room, card and supper rooms. Card tables can be placed in the drawing-room when a separate room for their use is not available.

Every giver of a ball looks forward to being repaid for the trouble and anxiety which it necessarily entails by the success of the entertainment. To ensure this there are one or two essential points which must be heeded. Of course, for the dance to be perfect, everything ought to be of the best— good room, good floor, good dancers, good music, and good supper; but it is impossible to compass the whole of this list in every case; therefore, the indispensables must be pointed out. We cannot alter the size and shape of our rooms, but one must be chosen as large as possible, and nearly square if possible, for a long narrow room is fatal to dancing; nor can we lay our floors afresh, but we need not fatigue our guests by obliging them to dance upon carpet. There can be no doubt that a polished floor, such as one meets with on the Continent, is the pleasantest and easiest to dance upon, but if our boards are rough ones, a brown-holland covering stretched tightly over them will be a good substitute for more substantial smoothness, if properly done, and is far preferable to another device which is sometimes most unwisely resorted to—viz., waxing the floor. A short time ago I was at a large ball in a county town where this was done, and the misery and vexation to which it gave rise were very great. Not only were our feet glued to the floor, to be severed only by a determined wrench at every step we took, but the destruction of dress was terrible—velvets, silks, and satins were quite spoilt by the wax which adhered to them; and no doubt many were the secret tears shed that night when the fair wearers laid them by.

Good dancers, too, it is not within the power of any hostess to command. She can only invite people who dance—she cannot ensure their dancing well. She must invite many guests, too, to fill her rooms, and those who dance well are few. This accomplishment is acquired to a certain degree by every girl, but whether it is that the other sex are constitutionally *gauche*, or that they have not been vouchsafed the same opportunities, we will not decide; certain it is that "bad partners" are more frequently complained of by the ladies than by the gentlemen—

> "Her feet beneath her petticoat
> Like little mice peeped in and out,
>   As if they feared the light;
> And oh! she dances such a way
> No sun upon an Easter day
>   Were half so fine a sight."

And now read a general description of a gentleman dancing the lancers*—

"Her partner has never spoken during the first

---

* *Saturday Review.*

four figures. He has no *memoria technica* to help him. When he valses he counts aloud. His ideas are beginning to desert him, and he is pushed into the middle as some kind of bewildering music commences. He remembers that there are two women in pink and one in blue who belong to his set, but the nondescript appearance of the fourth upsets all his calculations. He runs about aimlessly, is found advancing with four girls, now giving both his hands to one of his own sex, now standing motionless on a dress. The result is disastrous, and he emerges out of the slough of despond bewildered and haggard."

Good music is a *sine quâ non*. If this be not secured—no matter whether the entertainment be what is called a "dance" or a "ball"—it will certainly be a failure. The want of it destroys all chance of enjoyment. It is impossible to dance well to bad music. "Bad music" means uneven, uncertain playing, and this is sure to be the result when amateurs attempt to play for dancers. Then, too, it is unfair to impose such a laborious and monotonous task on your guests. If the party is to be a small one, have a proficient man or woman to play the piano; if it be a large one, then one or two instruments as well as the piano are necessary, such as violin, cornet, or harp, varied by the addition of bells and triangles. The place in the room that these musicians should occupy is a difficult matter to decide. They always seem in the way. The saying about children, that they should be seen and not heard, should be reversed, if possible, with this band of musicians. They should be heard but not seen; or at any rate their bodily presence should not be obtrusive. The best plan we have seen is to place a little wooden hut outside the windows of the dancing room, and take out the window frame, at the same time screening it as much as possible with evergreens, ferns, and flowers; but of course this is not always practicable, for several reasons.

The supper has been treated of in another chapter, so we will only emphasise the necessity for substantiality as well as elegance, and pass on to other details.

All the rooms in the house should be brilliantly lighted, for light induces gaiety and mirth. Darkness engenders silence and gloom. The illumination of the ball-room is another difficulty which besets the giver of dances, especially if the house be a country one. Gas makes a room very hot and oppressive, no doubt, but it is the easiest and most effectual mode of lighting a room, if it is available, and good ventilation can do much to remedy the evils it carries with it. Wax candles are objectionable on these occasions, because, fanned and irritated by the continual motion of the dancers, they drop their waxy tears on coat and dress, the traces of which remain for ever and a day. French lamps, placed on brackets at short distances, and high enough to be out of the way, shed the softest and most pleasing light. If the dance is of long duration, the lamps may require to be re-trimmed one by one during the course of the evening, or darkness will perchance descend upon the scene.

There cannot be too great a display of flowers. The fireplaces should be screened with them or with large ferns, so filled as to resemble a garden bank. The mantelpieces may be covered with small tin trays, containing flowers. Console tables, or any other flat surface, may be decorated in like manner; and on the staircase, below the banister, flowers are often arranged so as to appear as if growing there. In fact, the whole should resemble as near as may be the ball-rooms in France during the luxurious age of the famed Louis Quatorze, of which we read that "perfumes exhaled from a thousand aromatic lamps, fragrant exotics filled the air with their sweet scents, while music soft and low breathed from a band of unseen minstrels."

A broad piece of carpet should be unrolled from the hall door to the carriage steps; and where the distance between the two is great, an awning should be stretched over the passage. As the guests arrive, they are ushered into the cloak-rooms. A maid should be at her post in that reserved for ladies, to give her aid in straightening dresses, arranging hair, and removing all trace of the slight disorder caused by the carriage drive. She should be armed with needle and thread to sew up the inevitable tears and rents which occur during the evening's campaign. It is also well to number hats, shawls, and cloaks, that they may be restored as quickly as possible to their owners on their departure. The lady having put a finishing touch to her hair, and the gentleman to his tie, the two are next conducted to the tea-room. Here a table is laid out with tea and coffee, cakes and biscuits, the beverages being dispensed by a servant. After having partaken of a cup of one or other, the new arrivals emerge from this room and are then shown into the drawing-room, where the lady of the house receives her guests Dancing should begin directly there is a sufficient number of people present to make a respectable show. In quadrilles and other square dances, those couples who are at the top of the room always begin the figure.

The different members of the family should all unite in trying to secure the pleasure of their guests, by noting those who are comparative strangers, and introducing them to partners, rather giving up their own than allowing their guests to feel themselves neglected. It is considered to be the duty of the son of the house to dance with each lady, and the daughter must not be partial, nor ever refuse to accept as a partner any guest of her father's for at least one dance. A lady and gentleman of my acquaintance went not long ago to a private ball, and, as it happened, found themselves strangers to all present. This need have been no drawback, if their entertainers had done their parts well; but as it was, they were left entirely to themselves, and not introduced to anybody. So they danced with one another, went by themselves to supper, and then went home deeply and justly annoyed by the want of thought, to designate it by no harsher name, displayed by their host and hostess and their sons and daughters. Such neglect is unpardonable.

The tea-room can be used as a refreshment-room; if possible, it should be on the same floor as the dancing-room. The table should be well supplied with ices and cups of claret, cider, and champagne; lemonade, sherry, coffee, small cakes, biscuits, and wafers. Two or three servants should be in constant attendance.

The fashion of programmes has become almost obsolete at the best London balls, which is a pity, as they were not only pretty *souvenirs* of the balls of a season, but also most convenient aids to memory at the time being; for if a girl has many partners it is no easy matter for her to remember to whom she is engaged for each dance. However, the capricious goddess for the time wills it otherwise, and only at country balls are programmes still found to survive.

It is considered "bad manners" if a man fails to come and claim his partner when the dance is about to commence, or for the lady to break her promise by accepting any other partner who may have asked for the pleasure of the same dance in the interim.

If a lady declines to dance with any one who may request her, but with whom she does not wish to become acquainted, and has no plea of a former engagement to offer for her refusal, the best course to take is, not to dance that particular dance at all, and then any chance of hurting the feelings of the rejected one is avoided.

The number of times that a lady should dance with the same partner, except under special circumstances, should be limited. Never so often as either to attract observation, or to call forth remarks on the subject.

After a dance the gentleman asks his partner whether she will take any refreshment, and if she replies in the affirmative he escorts her to the room and procures her an ice, offers to hold a cup for her, and when the music for the next dance begins he conducts her to her chaperon, when she disengages herself from his arm, they bow to one another, and he leaves her. It is not customary to promenade much after a dance.

Private balls usually begin at ten p.m., and end about three a.m.; supper at one a.m.

The gentleman with whom the lady has been last dancing generally takes her in to supper.

It is necessary to bid good-night to your hostess, but you go away quietly, that your departure may not be noticed, lest it should tend to break up the party.

In the foregoing pages, public and private balls on a large scale have been described. The entertainments known by the name of "Cinderella Dances" are of a less elaborate and expensive character. They originated from the desire of young people to meet frequently for the pleasure of dancing. A "Cinderella Dance" begins at eight p.m., and ends as the clock strikes the hour of midnight—hence the origin of the title. No supper is provided or expected; refreshments such as coffee, tea, biscuits, and claret only, are set on the tables.

CHAPTER XV.

PRIVATE THEATRICALS.

Amateur Acting—Charades—Tableaux Vivants—Wax-Work Exhibitions—Private Theatricals.

> "And then, and much it helped his chance—
> He could sing and play first fiddle and dance,
> Perform charades and proverbs of France."
>
> *Hood.*

CHARADES, *tableaux vivants*, wax-work exhibitions, and private theatricals are excellent amusements for winter evenings, and more especially for households in the country, where all the excitement must be provided within doors. There are many occasions where the want is felt of some fresh enlivenment. Dancing night after night becomes monotonous, but acting is always interesting, and it provides occupation and amusement for the daytime also, in the preparation of dresses and scenes and the learning and rehearsal of parts. This taste for amateur acting has spread so rapidly that it would seem as if the rising generation of this country would resemble the Greeks, and be "one entire nation of actors and actresses."

A paterfamilias who is blessed with a quiver full of olive-branches, being thus provided with a sufficient company for his domestic stage, may cast a play to his own liking without having the trouble to go abroad for his theatrical amusements.

As an American writer* well remarks, "It is pleasant to see and hear real gentlemen and ladies, who do not think it necessary to mouth and rant and stride, like too many of our stage heroes and heroines, in the characters which show off their graces and talents; and most of all, to see a fresh, unrouged, unspoiled, high-bred young maiden, with a lithe figure and a pleasant voice, acting in those love dramas that make us young again to look upon, when real youth and beauty will play them for us."

Charades are the easiest of these three amusements, both to act and to arrange. They can be got up in a very short space of time—indeed, they are often the best when quite impromptu. They are a great help in entertaining a room full of promiscuous people. In the country, where friends and neighbours are invited to tea and supper, it often happens that midway between the two the evening begins to "drag," as the term is. Perhaps the majority of the guests do not care for music. The conversation grows slow and faint. What can the hostess do to revive the drooping spirits of the party? Charades are the very kind of excitement required to infuse life and merriment into the dejected, silent company. No special talent is needed. A few of the young people are despatched into another room to arrange the charade. A word of two or three syllables is chosen, of which each syllable is a word of itself, and is acted as such. For instance, the word "infantry" might be

---

* O. W. Holmes.

selected. There would be a scene for each syllable—an inn, we will say, an evening party, and a village school, and the whole word represented by a regiment of soldiers. Someone should be placed at the head of this band as leader, who will urge decision on the word to be chosen, and suggest the characters to be adopted, and by whom they are to be personated; otherwise much time will be spent in useless discussion, and those who await the return of the actors into the drawing-room will grow weary. Then as to the dresses, they are selected out of those hastily collected together; and quick wits will soon convert a few shawls, cloaks, &c., into most wonderful and imposing costumes. Great results are attained by the means of wigs, spectacles, and burnt cork. The more complete the transformation the greater the fun—gentlemen dressed as ladies, children metamorphosed into adults, thin people made up into stout ones—any change, in fact, but that of ladies donning male attire. The drawing-room is the scene of action. One end of it is arranged for what it is to represent, as cleverly as means at command and time will allow, and then the actors troop in and begin to represent the scene chosen in the best way that they can by their words and actions. The chief actor should keep his eye on his subordinates during the performance; he should move about and keep up the conversation, as there should never be a pause; and when he sees their inventive powers begin to flag, he should retire with his company in as natural a manner as possible. The scenes should not be of long duration, and the amateurs should have all their wits about them, to make the conversation as smart as possible;

never be tongue-tied or nervous; and, above all, they must have their risible muscles well under command, so that if one of their companions raises a laugh amongst the audience, either by grotesque appearance or lively sallies, the other actors must not be tempted to join. Indeed, those who wish to act well must throw themselves entirely into their characters. Charades are frequently performed in dumb-show.

Tableaux vivants require more time and care in the arrangements. It is possible to get them up hastily; but to be really effective, rehearsals are requisite. As the name denotes, they are pictures merely, and therefore the costume and the position are all that there is to study. The best plan is to select some well-known painting, either with one or several figures in it, and copy it as closely in dress and attitude as may be, or a scene out of a book or play. "Fortitude," one of Sir J. Reynolds' paintings; Paul de la Roche's "Marie Antoinette returning from the Revolutionary Tribunal;" "Reading the Newspaper," by Sir David Wilkie; Ary Scheffer's well-known "St. Augustine with his mother, Ste. Monica," are good subjects for representation. "King Alfred in the Neatherd's Cottage," "The Princes in the Tower," "The Nobles offering the Crown to Lady Jane Grey," and many other historical subjects, might be selected. Good illustrated editions of Shakespeare and other standard books furnish an ample field for choice; but care should be taken to select subjects which differ as widely as possible one from the other in character, as the striking contrasts presented by varied *tableaux* add greatly to the general effect. The figure or group should be placed exactly like the original, and should remain motionless—we might say breathless —for the few moments during which the audience are permitted to gaze upon the living picture. *Tableaux* should be acted in a room that has folding doors. These should be put back or taken off the hinges, and a pair of curtains, which can be drawn at the sides like window curtains, be arranged across the opening; for drapery arranged in this manner adds greatly to the effect of the picture. Behind these curtains stretch coarse green tarlatan, doubled. This subdues and softens the light, which ought to come from the side. The background of the picture should be dark, so as to throw out the figures in front. A large folding screen, covered with some dark material, will answer this purpose.

A wax-work exhibition is a species of *tableaux vivants* which is now frequently acted. People are dressed to represent different characters, and are placed on an improvised platform, or in niches, corners, window recesses, and different parts of a room, into which the spectators are brought to see the show. There should be someone well qualified to describe each figure. After this has been done, the exhibitor proceeds to wind up the figures by clock-work. This idea is conveyed by winding a watchman's rattle slowly, or some other such device. Each figure should then move some part of the body slowly, and with a slightly spasmodic action.

Private theatricals require more talent than either of the two kinds of acting that we have described, in that the actors have to learn their parts by heart. Many rehearsals are necessary, and much patience and perseverance are needful if the performance is to be a success. They need not be costly entertainments; and when well carried out, none give greater pleasure and amusement to all concerned. It is absolutely necessary that a commander-in-chief should be appointed, one who will direct and supervise the whole affair. Amateur actors are apt to be very enthusiastic at first, and eagerly take the parts assigned to them (a very delicate task, by the way, that of apportioning to each one the *rôle* which he or she is to play); they begin industriously to learn their parts, repeat them with great zest at the first rehearsal, and then too often their zeal abates, and idleness creeps over them, and the whipper-in has no small task in urging them to complete the work begun, and to make another effort with the half-learned part, which at present the prompter has to repeat almost verbatim.

Our early ancestors strewed their stages with rushes, and before each act hung up the *name* of the scene in lieu of the scene itself; but such simplicity does not content us. We should deem so primitive a performance very tame and uninteresting. If the entertainment is to be carried out to perfection, all that requires to be done in the way of scenery and dresses is to write to a London decorator and costumier, mentioning the plays that are to be acted, and they will make all the necessary arrangements for fitting up and providing scenery and dresses. Every detail will be attended to; all difficulties will vanish. The following suggestions, though somewhat theoretical and ideal, might, we think, be made practicable, and, if so, would add greatly to the *tout ensemble*. "The stage scenery, orchestra, &c., should be planned on a model new, original, and peculiar to themselves, so distinguished from our public theatres that they should not strike the eye like a copy in miniature, but as the independent sketch of a master who disdains to copy. Many noble halls and stately apartments in the great houses and castles of our nobility would give an artist ample field for fancy. Halls and saloons, flanked with interior columns, and surrounded by galleries, would, with the aid of proper draperies or scenery in the intercolumniations, take a rich and elegant appearance; and at the same time the music might be so disposed in the gallery as to produce a most animating effect."

The same writer also suggests that the play itself should only be a part of the entertainment, woven into a grand *fête*, and that the spectators should not be left to doze in their seats, but be called upon in the intervals, by music, dance, and refreshment, to change the sameness of the scene. If, on the other hand, the expense of hiring the portable theatre is an obstacle, or the distance from town is too great, then the inventive faculties must be set to work to supply the many requisites in scenery and dress. "C'est des difficultés que naissent des miracles" (out of difficulties grow miracles), says La Bruyère.

With the help of a carpenter great things may be effected. The stage should be a platform, raised some distance from the floor, and if possible should slope slightly from back to front. A strip of board a few inches high should run along the edge, at the back of which are placed the footlights. For these lights gas can be easily laid on from the nearest pipe. If that convenience is not within reach, then small oil-lamps or candles must supply the want. Two curtains will answer the purpose of a drop scene. These should be long and wide enough to cover the whole front of the stage when let down, and of some heavy texture. The proper working of these curtains should be well ascertained beforehand, or they are likely to cause awkward dilemmas when they do not fall and rise instantaneously. The method to be adopted is to fasten two cords where the two curtains meet in the centre, and work them over hooks placed on the top corners right and left. These cords should be fastened to the curtains at intervals of a foot.

If modern plays are acted, not much stage scenery need be used. The side screens can be made of frames of wood covered with canvas. Doors and windows can also be easily formed in the same way. A great deal can be done with screens.

In most play-books there is a full description of the scenery required and the dresses requisite for the different characters.

If the play chosen be one representing life in bygone days, the costumes will be more difficult to prepare at home, for so much satin, velvet, gold and silver lace as our gaily, richly-clothed ancestors wore do not generally form part of our possessions. Dresses of this kind it is better to hire from a costumier. It is wonderful, however, what study and thought can produce, and what brilliant ideas spring up when one is forced by necessity to invent something. I read the other day an account of some theatricals acted on board ship a thousand miles from any shop, so wits were forced to devise, and did devise, wonders. "Once," says the writer (Lady Barker), " we manufactured some large silver buttons for an old-fashioned coat out of the round pieces of white metal which cover the corks of soda-water bottles; we polished them up till they shone brightly. Then we cut them into shape, and punched a couple of holes in the centre, which made them at once brilliant and beautiful buttons, all ready to be sewed on. Upon the same occasion we required a 'black lutestring figured blue.' This nearly drove us distracted; for although there were dozens of old black silk dresses on board, not one had any figures. At last the happy idea came into someone's head to borrow a set of paste cutters from the cook and some light blue tissue paper from the steward. We stamped out a number of little shamrocks with one of the cutters, and then pasted them all over the silk gown. The effect was beautiful. Beards and wigs we made out of unravelled yarn. They looked rather too curly, but we powdered them well with flour."

CHAPTER XVI.

GARDEN PARTIES.

> "What sport shall we devise here in the garden
> To drive away the heavy thought of care?
> Madam, we'll play at bowls;
> Madam, we'll dance."
> *Richard II.*

THE chief thing required to make a garden party enjoyable is fine weather, a bright, sunshiny, calm day, when the mere pleasure of being out of doors almost compensates for the lack of other adjuncts. This special enjoyment we cannot insure for our guests, but there are other pleasures which lie within our compass of provision. See that the gardens and grounds are in perfect order—not a leaf to be seen on the neatly-cut, freshly-rolled lawns and walks; not a single weed in the trim flower-beds. Tents of various picturesque forms can be erected here and there for refreshments; a small band of musicians with stringed instruments, or a company of glee-singers hidden from general view, can discourse sweet music at intervals, and enliven the scene. A lawn-tennis ground (two or more such spaces if possible) should be provided for the amusement of tennis players, of whom in the present day there are always a considerable number amongst garden-party guests. Tea, coffee, and cakes of many kinds should be in readiness for the guests on their arrival, and later, these should be replaced by ices, claret-cup, strawberries, grapes, peaches, melons, and the like.

The greater number of people invited to a garden party the better. Then friends meet friends—a desirable end, as introductions are not made.

As soon as the guests arrive they are conducted to the garden, where they find the hostess near the entrance of the garden or some particular tent —any place that is a convenient position for receiving her visitors before they pass on and mingle with the other guests. The hostess has no onerous duties to perform on an occasion of this kind, as no introductions are made. Having received her guests, she is permitted to desert her post and enjoy the company of her friends, unfettered by the thought of any duty, except the pleasant one of saying a few words to each one of her guests; nor need she be disturbed for the bidding of *adieux*, a formality which is not required at these informal gatherings.

There is a duty which devolves upon the host or upon the son of the house; failing these, it must be undertaken by a specially-appointed friend, or by a daughter of the house. This duty is to direct in some measure the games on the tennis-lawn. Many tennis parties are dull and spiritless owing to this want of supervision. It is essential that a chief should arrange sets, should go about amongst the guests—who, if they are players, are generally to be found watching the games—and ask them if they have played, or would like to do so. Guests who are strangers to each other often do not come forward to arrange games, and thus it sometimes happens that the ground is unused for a length of time, although there are numbers of ladies all the while longing to play; and it also sometimes happens that one set of tennis players take possession of a ground, and play set after set, to the exclusion of other players. These drawbacks to general enjoyment can and should be prevented.

Garden parties begin about four o'clock, and unless mention is especially made of dancing, the company separates between seven and eight.

It is well to specify on the card of invitation the nature of the entertainment, in order that the guests may be attired accordingly. At the *fêtes champêtres* given by Queen Anne, the guests were expected to sail about in full dress; and as a view of the Broad Walk at Kensington, which was the favourite promenade, could be commanded from Hyde Park, the poor commonalty could have a peep, and could criticise the high-born guests who glided about the garden in "brocaded robes, hoops, fly-caps, and fans."

The present fashion is to wear morning dress, but as picturesque as you please; indeed, the ladies should look like butterflies fluttering about; if archery is to be the amusement, a different costume is required from that worn for lawn-tennis; and if a dance is to end the day, then the style of dress would again be altered, though it would never diverge into "full dress." When the sun shows his face, a garden party is one of the prettiest sights imaginable—the smooth green turf, with its bright bordering of flowers; the gaily-dressed company reposing under shady trees, pacing the sward, darting hither and thither on the lawn-tennis ground, or displaying their prowess at the target, the whole

> "Canopied by the blue sky,
> So cloudless, pure, and beautiful."

If this entertainment be a country one, the guests adjourn to the house at sunset, and there partake of a substantial supper, after which they drive home; or the day is concluded by a moonlight dance on the lawn, or in one of the tents, and the garden and grounds are sometimes illuminated with Chinese lanterns and small coloured lamps hung in festoons from the trees, which make the evening scene as picturesque as that of the morning.

CHAPTER XVII.

EXCURSIONS AND PICNICS.

Why People enjoy Picnics—Private Picnics—Conveyance of Guests and of Provisions—Subscription Picnic · Election and Duties of a Manager—Things not to be forgotten—Provisions and Beverages—Tea.

> "Nor rural sights alone, but rural sounds,
> Exhilarate the spirit, and restore
> The tone of languid nature."
> *Cowper.*

> "The days when we went a-gypsying,
> A long time ago."
> *Old Song.*

THERE are plenty of people who enjoy picnics besides the children for whose benefit they are generally supposed to be arranged. Rural sights and rural sounds, when all nature is alive and gay in the glad summer time, have a happy and genial effect on the most misanthropical of persons; then, too, the absence of all state and ceremony, the liberty, the entire change and freedom from etiquette, conduce to gaiety of spirit and mirth. After all, it is the novelty which is the great charm, for the same set of people whom you now see making merry over the salt and the sugar having fraternised by the way, and who now declare it to be the summit of human felicity to sit in an uncomfortable position upon something never intended to be a seat, beside a table-cloth which, being spread upon an uneven and elastic surface, causes everything that should remain perpendicular to assume a horizontal attitude—these same people would grumble loudly did such things occur daily. At the end of a week they would be seriously annoyed and put out of temper by the reappearance of the inevitable frog which they now laugh at so heartily as it hops across the table-cloth, and, losing its presence of mind on finding itself so suddenly launched into fashionable life, seeks refuge in the heart of a pigeon pie. Such little *contretemps* add immensely to the liveliness and hilarity of a picnic, because, coming but once in a way, they can hardly be looked upon as discomforts.

It might be imagined that as a picnic is a kind of scramble, there can be but few arrangements to make, but in reality an excursion of this kind entails much labour and thought on the "getters-up." There are private picnics and subscription ones. Speaking of the former, the first thing to plan, after the place is fixed upon, must be how to convey your guests there. If possible, they should go in different ways; some in carriages of various descriptions, large wagonettes being the pleasantest; some on horseback; some by boat, it may be; but never in a long procession, reminding one of the string of vans full of children, or members of various benefit clubs going to Epping Forest or Bushey Park for the day, who wave their pocket-handkerchiefs at each passer-by in a friendly way, and are never weary of the perpetual twang of the two or three instruments which accompany them. We have known pleasant parties to be arranged by railway, when a saloon carriage has been engaged for the occasion, although the very name seems to put an end to all idea of rural enjoyment.

The provisions should have a separate vehicle allotted to them, and not be scattered about in the different carriages, a basket stowed away in one corner, a hamper thrust under another seat, and so forth. No; a light cart is the best kind of conveyance for the delicacies. There are now very convenient hampers made for the better packing and conveying of provisions to these *al fresco* entertainments, so that the pies and the patties do not present such a depressed appearance as heretofore, and the cayenne is not so likely to mingle indiscriminately with things in general, and the sweets in particular, as "in the days when *we* went gypsying." The meats, pies, &c., should all be wrapped in clean cloths. The servants—not too many, please, or we shall have too much state and ceremony—accompanying the cart should start in good time, so as to be at the destination when the company arrives, for it is best to dine or tea, whichever it may be, immediately, and disperse at pleasure afterwards. If children have a voice in the matter, tea is chosen, for the delight of making the fire is intense, in spite of the blinding, suffocating smoke which is the invariable accompaniment. At the end of the chapter will be found a list of things which may be taken to a picnic. Of course, all the provisions are cooked beforehand, except it may be that potatoes are roasted, or, if possible, a dish of hot fish is prepared on the spot.

When a subscription picnic is decided upon, a manager or manageress should be elected, and he or she should devise a plan for equally dividing the duty of providing, and also of sharing the responsibilities of the day. Unless this is done, the greatest confusion will ensue, for people's ideas run singularly in one direction. When the time arrives for unpacking the baskets, it will be found that everybody has brought forks, and no one has thought of spoons; pigeon pies—which seem associated in everybody's mind with picnics—will come out of every hamper, while the plainer and more substantial dishes, such as lamb and beef, have not been remembered. A list should be made and given to each contributor a few days beforehand of things for which he or she will be held responsible, and this should be so arranged that each should bring some of the crockery or glass, as well as eatables. It is also better that one person should provide all that is required of one kind, than that several should be supplied by the same individual. For instance, one person might be asked to contribute all the fruit as their share, and be responsible for the appearance of all the plates required; another supply the joints of meat, together with knives and forks; a third, the pastry and the glass; another, the rolls of bread, cheese, and the silver, and so on. The gentlemen of the party generally contribute the beverages, and they might have their division—one bring sherry, another the bottled beer, a third soda-water, and so on. Two or three corkscrews ought to be taken, and a small gong is useful to collect the party together, either for the meal itself or the departure. Mint sauce and salad dressing in bottles, pounded sugar, and the other condiments, mustard, salt, and pepper, should be particularly remembered.

For an out-door luncheon, the following list of

provisions will be found the most suitable :—Cold roast beef, ribs and shoulder of lamb, roast fowls, ducks, ham, pressed tongue; beefsteak, pigeon, and grouse pies, game, veal patties, lobsters, cucumbers and lettuces for salad, cheese-cakes, jam or marmalade turnovers, stewed fruit in bottles, bottle of cream, college puddings, blancmange in mould, plain biscuits to eat with fruit and cheese, rolls, butter, cream cheese, and fresh fruit. Bottled beer and porter, claret, sherry, champagne, soda-water, lemonade, cherry-brandy.

For tea :—Loaves of bread, sponge-cakes, plum-cakes, buns, rolls, butter, potted fish and meats, tongue, cheese-cakes, plain and sweet biscuits, fruits, bottle of cream, and tea. It is useless to attempt to make coffee on an occasion of this kind, unless the company is capable of appreciating the fragrant berry in its best form, *i.e.*, Turkish coffee, which can be made to perfection in an ordinary saucepan, wherein it should be allowed just to come to boiling point three times in succession, and then served while the rich brown foam is still on the surface.

CHAPTER XVIII.

FIELD SPORTS AND AMUSEMENTS.

Field Sports—Hunting—Shooting—Fishing—Boating—
Tricycling—Skating.

> "We'll make you some sport with the fox
> Ere we case him."
> *All's Well that Ends Well.*

> "God made the country and man made the town."
> *Cowper.*

"MENS sana in corpore sano," Juvenal tells us, is the greatest gift bestowed by the gods, and modern science has proved clearly enough that the body acts on the mind as well as *vice versâ*—that our mental faculties are seldom able fully to develop themselves into perfect action unless the body be in a healthy state.

Now we do not intend to enter into a learned disquisition as to all the means by which these crazy frames of ours are kept in good repair, but to assert boldly that one great aid towards preserving them in proper order lies in the judicious use of field sports and amusements.

Corroding, carking care vanishes into thin air when the ardent lover of these pursuits gives himself thoroughly up for the nonce to the enjoyment of them. What more exhilarating sound than the sonorous yelping of the hounds giving tongue, or the yet more joyful shout, "Gone away!"—

> "When a southerly wind and a cloudy sky
> Proclaim it a hunting morning."

What town-wearied man does not feel refreshed and reinvigorated as he climbs the hills with a gun on his shoulder and a dog at his heels? and for the time being is not his one wish—

> "Give me the naked heavens above,
> The broad bare heath below"?

The angler, boater, and skater each experiences keen enjoyment from his own particular pastime. Field sports have always proved the best corrector of that "effeminacy which refined luxury is apt to produce," and it is a happy circumstance when a taste prevails for such amusements as, while they add grace, health, and vigour to the body, have "no tendency to enfeeble and corrupt the mind."

The sport *par excellence* of the Englishman is hunting, and the English are the only nation who will ride hard at the chase. Dr. Johnson, who followed the fox with as much glee as anybody, says a Frenchman goes out upon a managed horse, and capers in the field, and no more thinks of jumping a hedge than of mounting a breach; and he relates an anecdote of a certain Lord Powerscourt who laid a wager in France that he would ride a great many miles in a certain short space of time. Thereupon it appears the French Academicians set to work, and calculated that from the resistance of the air it was an impossibility! However, his English lordship performed the feat.

Nor is this sport confined to gentlemen alone. Many a fair lady may be seen on her well-groomed, glossy-coated hunter, following the hounds.

At one period the chase of the stag was highly popular in Britain, and our countrywomen had hunting expeditions on their own account. Sketches of these "fast" ladies are by no means rare. I have seen one copied from a manuscript of the fourteenth century, which depicts a huntress seated astride on her palfrey, and blowing a horn to cheer her dog and stimulate her archeress. The latter answers the call by planting an arrow between the horns of a stag.

And at a later date Englishwomen still continued to attend the chase. Our good Queen Bess was a lover of this sport; and Queen Anne was an indefatigable huntress, so much so that when her failing health obliged her to discontinue equestrian exercise, she followed the chase in a light one-horse chaise in which she had been known to drive herself forty and fifty miles during the day.

When the stag was brought to bay it was considered a mark of gallantry on the part of one of the hunters to offer the fatal weapon to some fair huntress, who thus had the privilege of cutting the deer's throat, a feat which required not only a sharp double-edged hunting-knife, but a steady arm and strong nerve, for it was a task by no means devoid of danger. In the "Bride of Lammermoor" we read, "It was not without a feeling bordering upon contempt that the enthusiastic hunter observed Lucy Ashton refused the hunter's knife presented to her, for the purpose of making the first incision into the stag's breast, and thereby discovering the quality of the venison."

Our fair sisters of the present day are not guilty of such sanguinary deeds, but show their bravery by leaping ditch and hedge, and often being "in at the death," and so receiving as a tribute of praise the brush of Master Reynard from the hands of some gallant gentleman of the hunt.

A lady's hunting dress is plain and useful, but a very becoming one withal. It consists of a dark-coloured tight-fitting habit, made with a very short skirt, or it will get sadly bespattered with mud. A plain linen collar is worn round the throat, fastened by a stud. Linen cuffs and tan-leather gloves finish the costume. The description of hat worn is a matter of choice. Some ladies wear the high-crowned beaver, and some prefer the low-crowned felt hat. Of late years, many ladies have taken to wear "pink" coats fashioned on the lines of a man's hunting coat; and very smart the scarlet coat looks with a dark habit skirt. Others are satisfied with a scarlet waistcoat, and in any case where a coat is worn the greatest care must be taken as to the proper tying of the hunting scarf that should finish off the neck. Sometimes when ladies have exhibited their "straight riding" for a certain length of time with a pack of hounds, the master will present them with "the button" of the hunt, and then they are entitled to wear the colours of that particular hunt—say a blue coat with buff facings, or dark green and scarlet, as the case happens to be.

The gentlemen's dress depends upon the fashion of the particular hunt of which they are members, as each has its peculiar costume; but the ordinary dress of a hunting man is either a scarlet or a dark-green coat, cut square (for the swallow-tail is obsolete), knee-breeches made of white or drab "cords," top-boots, and a tall hat, or a cap of black velvet, with a small stiff peak. Spurs must not be forgotten, and a scarf of cashmere, fastened by a pin, will be found more convenient wear and look more suitable than a tie. But it is not proper for a man to appear in "pink" or green, unless he is a regular member of some hunt, and is a *bonâ fide* hunting man, who means to ride straight across country.

The place appointed for the "meet" is duly advertised in the newspapers. The first and last of the season generally take place at the residence of the master of the hounds. Our forefathers threw off the pack as soon as they could distinguish a stile from a gate. They had six o'clock breakfasts; while we, more indolent and luxurious, do not dream of appearing at the rendezvous before ten a.m., and after a hard day's run are quite ready for a hearty dinner at eight p.m.

Shooting parties are organised as follows:— The gentlemen, habited in rough, thick coats, knickerbockers, thick stockings and leggings, and substantial boots, start, after a hearty breakfast, with dogs and keepers to shoot grouse, partridge, or pheasant, as the case may be. Some convenient place is appointed whereat to meet for luncheon, and to this spot the ladies of the household often repair, and a very pleasant hour is spent in discussing game-pie, patties, and cold beef, beer, and champagne, at these *al fresco* luncheons. After an hour's chat, and the consumption of a cigar or so, the gentlemen resume their work of destruction, and the ladies either watch them at a respectful distance or drive homewards. If they choose the former alternative, they should take great care not to wander away. On a moor there is not so much danger of accidents happening in this way, but when pheasant-shooting is the sport we think that ladies are better out of the way, unless they are very tractable, and obediently follow close on the track of the sportsmen.

"Fishing, and particularly that branch of it called angling, calls forth considerable powers of invention and much dexterity of practice," says the "Angler's Guide." Every year the number of lady-anglers increases, and some of the best records in salmon-fishing on the Scotch rivers are annually made by women. A kilt skirt of rough tweed unhemmed, and reaching a little below the knee, over a pair of tweed knickerbockers to match, a Norfolk jacket with plenty of pockets, ribbed woollen stockings, stout low-heeled shoes, and a deerstalker cap, form the best and most workmanlike costume for a woman to go fishing in.

Fishing parties on the banks of some broad, deep, well-stocked river, where the fish are not too sensitive to the chatter and laughter of the anglers, may be made very enjoyable. A man should be taken for the purpose of baiting the hooks and taking off the fish when caught. Then, if the sport is good, the hours fly quickly and pleasantly by. Luncheon is brought, and if a fire can be made, and some of the freshly-caught fish cooked, the entertainment is complete. The gentlemen of the party should always be ready to lay down their rods and render help to any lady who may require it—in the matter of disentangling lines, re-arranging floats, putting together rods.

In boating, gentlemen should always attend to

the comfort as well as the safety of ladies who may place themselves under their protection. One gentleman should stay in the boat and do his best to steady it, while the other helps the ladies to step from the bank. They should then be comfortably seated, and their dresses arranged so as to be in no danger of getting wet, before a start is made. As the seat of honour in a boat is that occupied by the stroke oar, it is etiquette for the owner of the boat to offer it to his friend should he be a rower.

Cycling is a much more modern pastime than those hitherto mentioned. It is an amusement the fashion for which has ebbed and flowed during the last ten years. Latterly, the various superior inventions amongst the machines which have been brought forward have fanned the flame of enthusiasm, and cycling has become one of the chief diversions of the day, and one in which ladies now join. A medical authority of high standing gives it as his opinion that exercise of this kind is equally beneficial to both sexes, and expresses a hope that this amusement will soon become as popular among ladies as tennis and the dance. A lady's tricycling dress consists of a plain skirt, made sufficiently wide to allow the feet free play without causing them to draw up the dress by their action, and yet not so wide as to permit the skirt to hang in folds or flap in the wind. A Norfolk jacket, made to fit neatly but not tightly to the figure, cut low round the throat to allow the neck free action. Both skirt and jacket should be made of a woollen material, and one that is porous and of light weight. A soft silk handkerchief is worn round the neck, which will hide the absence of collar and brooch. Shoes, having firm but not heavy soles, and a close-fitting soft hat made of the same material as the dress, complete the costume. The dress for a gentleman is knickerbockers, and a short coat buttoned up the front; stockings ribbed, and knitted of thick wool; shoes with stout soles; a cap with peaks at the front and back, made, like the suit, of porous woollen material, or an ordinary straw hat. A light silk handkerchief loosely tied round the neck should take the place of a stiff collar and tie.

Skating is another amusement in which ladies join, and which in some parts of the country is looked forward to as a delightful certainty. A temperature below zero is hailed with delight, and the belles and the beaux alike hasten to "visit the icy scenes, and mock the terrors of the frost." In days of yore the maidens contented themselves with watching the skaters, but now they are as fleet as any Laplander or Hollander. "When the greate fenne or moore is frozen," says an old chronicler, describing a skating-scene in the vicinity of London, "many younge men play on the yce. Some stryding as wide as they may, doe slide swiftly. Some tye bones to their feete and under their heeles, and, shoving themselves by a little picked staffe, do slide as swiftly as a birde flyeth in the air or an arrow out of a crosse bow." A gentleman should carry the lady's skates if he be her walking companion. He will find her a chair, and fasten on her skates; guide, support, and instruct her at first if she be a novice in the art; and, in short, be as chivalrous in his behaviour as any knight in the olden time. The ladies, on their side, must not tax the patience of their instructors too severely.

It is sometimes days before they are able to stand upon their skates or dare to venture without a strong arm to lean upon for fear of a fall. Let them practise by themselves on some small pond, where a tumble will hurt neither them nor their modesty.

CHAPTER XIX.

THE COURT.

St. James's and Buckingham Palaces—Who may be Presented—Ladies' Court Dress—Gentlemen's Court Dress—Rules and Regulations—The Drawing-Room—The Levée—The Irish Court—Court Mourning.

> "—— let me kiss my Sovereign's hand,
> And bow my knee before his majesty."
> *Richard II.*

> "*2nd Gentleman*—You saw the ceremony?
> *3rd.*—That I did.
> *1st.*—How was it?
> *3rd.*—Well worth seeing.
> *2nd.*—Good Sir, speak it to us.
> *3rd.*—As well as I am able."
> *Henry VIII.*

THE extreme formality of Court etiquette, and the strict observance which must be paid to all its rules, will of necessity render this chapter of information regarding it a very precise and formal one.

The Queen now holds her drawing-rooms and levées at Buckingham Palace, the State apartments there being more spacious than those at St. James's Palace, where they were formerly held. Levées are still held at St. James's Palace by the Prince of Wales. This palace was originally a hospital for lepers. It was purchased by Henry VIII., who altered it, and made it as it now stands. After the destruction of the Palace of Whitehall, in 1695, St. James's became the town residence of our Sovereigns, and continued to be so up to the accession of our Queen in 1837, when the Court took up its abode at Buckingham Palace.

Ladies and gentlemen who wish to be presented to their Sovereign at a drawing-room or levée can only obtain the honour through one of their acquaintances who has previously been presented. It will be seen by the Lord Chamberlain's Regulations that the one who presents must also appear at Court as well as the one presented; so that this rule, together with other reasons, which may be easily divined, makes it a matter of delicacy for one person to ask the favour of another, unless they are relatives or very intimate friends. Her Majesty is graciously accessible to all persons of rank and title, provided they bear a good character in society; but it would be in vain for any lady to sue for admittance into the Courtly circle, however high her rank, if there were the least stain upon her reputation. The wives and daughters of the clergy, naval and military officers, of physicians, barristers, and bankers, may also be presented, provided their conduct is *sans reproche*.

The dress worn on these occasions, both by the ladies and gentlemen, has quite a distinctive feature of its own, and therefore the descriptions are placed in this chapter instead of that headed "The Toilet." The Court dress of the lady consists of petticoat, bodice, and train. The petticoat is of silk, with tulle or lace trimmings, made long, and is in reality like the skirt of an ordinary ball dress. The bodice, which is made quite low, with short sleeves, and of the same material as the petticoat, is trimmed to match that garment. The train is of great length and breadth, and is worn falling either from the waist or shoulders. It is made of a more costly and handsome material than the other part of the dress; velvet or satin is chosen, and it is trimmed with lace, and feathers or flowers to correspond. The head-dress consists of feathers and lace lappets, or a veil of white tulle, and the hair is ornamented with diamonds or other precious stones. The other portions of the costume—the shoes, the fan, and the gloves, which must be white—should all be consistent with "full dress."

As to the Court dress of the gentlemen, that which came to us in the days of the early Georges, the costume of Louis Quinze, remains for the most part as the Court dress of to-day.

This dress—which retains the main feature of the period of 1700—consists of coat and knee-breeches of plum-coloured cloth, ornamented with steel buttons; a white waistcoat, embroidered in colours; an elaborately frilled shirt; pink silk stockings; shoes with diamond or steel buckles; and a sword, which hangs suspended by a steel chain to the hilt. Lastly comes the cocked hat, and the outer man is complete.

Various attempts have been made to discard this dress, and of late years a newer style has been substituted, and instead of the plum-coloured cloth some gentlemen wear black silk velvet coat, breeches, and waistcoat, ornamented with gilt or silver buttons, with which the shoe-buckles and sword correspond. Naval and military men appear in their uniforms, bishops and dignitaries of the Church in their robes.

REGULATIONS TO BE OBSERVED AT THE QUEEN'S DRAWING ROOM AT BUCKINGHAM PALACE.

By her Majesty's command.—The ladies who propose to attend her Majesty's drawing-room at Buckingham Palace are requested to bring with them two large cards, with their names clearly written thereon; one to be left with the Queen's page in attendance in the corridor, and the other to be delivered to the Lord Chamberlain, who will announce the name to the Queen.

PRESENTATIONS.

Any lady who proposes to be presented must leave at the Lord Chamberlain's office, St. James's Palace, before twelve o'clock, two clear days previous to that on which the drawing-room is held, a card with her name written thereon, and one with the name of the lady by whom she is to be presented. In order to carry out the existing regulation, that no presentation can be made at a drawing-room excepting by a lady actually attending the Court, it is also necessary that an intimation from the lady who is to make the presentation of her intention to be present should accompany the presentation card above referred to, which will be submitted to the Queen for her Majesty's approbation. It is her Majesty's command that no presentation shall be made at the drawing-room except in accordance with the above regulations.

It is particularly requested that in every case the names be very distinctly written upon the cards to be delivered to the Lord Chamberlain, in order that there may be no difficulty in announcing them to the Queen.

It is not expected that gentlemen will present themselves at drawing-rooms, except in attendance upon the ladies of their families.

Any gentleman who, under these circumstances, should desire to be presented to the Queen will observe the same regulations as are in force for her Majesty's levées.

The State apartments will be open for the reception of the company coming to Court at two o'clock.

These regulations apply equally to gentlemen and ladies. Directions at what gate to enter, and where the carriages are to set down, are always printed in the newspapers.

The ceremony of presentation is as follows:—

On getting out of the carriage, everything in the shape of shawl or cloak is left behind. The train is carried over the left arm. When the lady's turn for presentation comes, she proceeds to the Presence Chamber or Throne Room, and on entering it lets down the train, which is instantly spread out by the lords-in-waiting with their wands. The card on which the lady's name is written is then handed to the Lord Chamberlain, who reads the name aloud to the Queen. The lady advances to the Queen, and when she arrives just before her Majesty curtseys very low, so low as *almost* to kneel to the Queen, who, if the lady presented be a peeress or a peer's daughter, kisses her forehead; but, in the case of a commoner, her Majesty holds out her hand to be kissed by the lady presented. The lady then rises, and making a curtsey to any members of the Royal Family who may be present, passes on, keeping her face towards the Queen, until she has passed out of the door appointed for those leaving the Presence Chamber.

The ceremony for gentlemen attending the Queen's levée is the same, with the exception that they kneel down on one knee on arriving before her Majesty, and kiss her hand. At levées held by the Prince of Wales the gentlemen bow and retire.

Presentations at the Irish Court differ in a few particulars of ceremony from those made at the English Court. Levées are held at the same time, but drawing-rooms take place in the evening at nine o'clock.

The same style of dress is required. The train is carried over the arm until the wearer reaches the Presence Chamber, when an aide-de-camp arranges the train. If the lady is *presented*, the Lord-Lieutenant kisses her cheek; she makes a curtsey and retires, but not backwards. If she is only attending the drawing-room, she curtseys and passes on.

The gentlemen attending the Lord-Lieutenant's levée bow on being presented. If any of those attending the drawing-room or levée are intimate with the Lord-Lieutenant, he shakes hands with them.

National mourning is ordered when a king or queen dies. The whole country is expected to show their respect in that way; but only black is required. The material is not specified, and crape is not worn. Until the present century, Court mourning for a king or queen in England was worn for a whole year as if for a parent. When the Court is ordered into mourning, on the death of any member or connection of the Royal Family, the dress required (which is generally of silk), and the length of time it is to be worn (usually three weeks), is published in the newspapers. "For the encouragement of our English silks," says a chronicler of Queen Anne's day, "his Royal Highness the Prince of Denmark and the nobility appear in mourning hatbands made of that silk, to bring the same into fashion, in the place of crapes, which are made in the Pope's country, whither we send our money for them."

CHAPTER XX.

DEATH.

Things to be done immediately upon a Death—Old Customs—The Funeral—The Mourners—The Service—Reading of the Will—Inquiries by Friends—Acknowledgment—The Sunday after the Funeral—Monuments.

> " The glories of our birth and state
> Are shadows, not substantial things.
> There is no armour against fate ;
> Death lays his icy hand on kings.
> Sceptre and crown
> Must tumble down,
> And in the dust be equal made
> With the poor crooked scythe and spade."
> *J. Shirley, 1620.*

THE "end of all things" is death. That stern reaper cuts down alike the bearded grain and the flowers that grow between. With his keen sickle he lays low old and young, the king and the peasant. All fall lifeless before him, and "their years come to an end as it were a tale that is told." When the dread moment has come and the spirit has taken its flight, some relative or friend undertakes to perform the necessary offices.

The coffin should be ordered without delay. It should be made of plain elm or oak, and lined with white jean. All the black, heathenish furniture with which coffins are often defaced should be discarded. The handles should either be plain rings of galvanised iron or of brass. At the lower end of the lid should be a white metal or brass plate, with the name, age, and date of death of the deceased.

Another immediate duty is to write to all relations and intimate friends and inform them of the death, and to send a notice of it for insertion in newspapers. This must be prepaid. The charge for such notice varies in different papers.

The arrangements for the funeral are generally directed by the head of the family, who expresses his wishes to an undertaker, and leaves the superintendence of the minor details in his hands. The love of parade and show which used to attend even these sad ceremonials has in a very great measure been put down by good taste; but it is advisable to be particularly explicit on that point, or the undertakers may carry out *their* ideas, which are too frequently for ostentatious display and the very reverse of simplicity.

Until very recently, it has been the general custom to supply crape scarfs and long crape hatbands to the mourners, and silk scarfs and hatbands, as well as gloves, to the friends, officiating clergymen, and bearers. At funerals of children and young girls, these scarfs were either of white silk, or of black silk tied with white ribbon. These special habiliments are now very rarely exhibited, and are rapidly falling into disuse.

About a hundred years ago the practice of laying the dead in state was very general, not for kings and great personages alone, but the bodies of merchants and tradesmen were also laid out amidst black velvet hangings. The coffin was surrounded by lighted candles, the doors of the houses were thrown open, and for several days the neighbours and general public were allowed to pass in and out to look at the corpse. Then after the funeral came the feast—for so the meal was called—of which all who had attended the funeral partook. Great numbers of friends and acquaintances were invited, sometimes as many as sixty or eighty to an ordinary funeral. Amongst the poor, the viands distributed at these feasts were cake and cheese, stewed prunes, and cold possets. The higher classes sat down to a dinner, which very often took place at an hotel.

There are many other customs which seem strange indeed to us now, and yet were in use in the last century, such as placing a plate of salt on the dead—salt being the emblem of eternity and immortality—carrying garlands of artificial flowers, intermixed with gilded empty egg-shells—emblems, it may be, of the hollowness of this life—before the funeral procession, and which were then hung in some conspicuous part of the church ; placing an hour-glass inside the coffin ; and one other singular custom, which, although savouring strongly of heathenish superstition, was observed in some nooks of England until quite lately, and that was as follows :— Poor people were hired to take upon them the sins of the deceased. When the corpse was brought out of the house and laid upon the bier, a loaf of bread, a mazard bowl full of beer, and a piece of money were delivered over the coffin to the sin-eater, who, in consideration of these gifts, took upon himself, *ipso facto*, all the sins of the defunct, and freed him or her from walking after death. Time has swept all these superstitious observances almost entirely away.

Hitherto it has not been usual for any of the female members of the family to attend the funeral, but if they feel strong enough, and can keep their grief within due bounds, let not the thought of what is customary prevent them from following their lost one to the grave, and from having the consolation of that most beautiful service of the Church for the burial of the dead. The dress of the chief mourners is, for ladies, woollen materials trimmed with crape—these are the only two materials worn at a funeral; and for gentlemen, black suits and ties, black kid gloves, and a band of black cloth round the hat.

At the time appointed, which is generally in the morning hours, those who are invited to attend the funeral proceed to the house. The invitations usually extend only to the particular friends of the deceased, and the family doctor and lawyer.

They assemble in the dining-room or library, when the undertaker gives a pair of gloves to each on his arrival. The ladies of the house do not appear until the mournful procession is ready to start, when they go direct from their own rooms to the mourning-coaches which are appointed to convey them. The nearest relatives of the deceased or representatives of the family follow, according to their degrees of kinship, next to the hearse, then the more distant ones, then friends, and often the procession is completed by the empty and closed carriages of acquaintances who are desirous to show their respect to the deceased and the bereaved family. The coffin is carried into the church and placed in the chancel. The funeral party have seats allotted to them in the same part. When the first part of the service is concluded, the clergyman proceeds to the grave, followed by the bearers and the mourners in the same order as they entered the church. When the last sad rite is ended, the group breaks up and disperses irregularly. The head of the family or its representative goes to the vestry to give the clergyman the particulars as to name and age, necessary for the filling up of the register, and also to pay the fees. The nominal fees differ in each parish. The expense of the grave depends upon whether a vault has been made, or whether it is a new grave. In reality, no fees are due of common right to the clergyman, but the immemorial custom of each parish has sanctioned the payment, so that they are always demanded. Three or four shillings is the stated fee, but well-to-do people generally give a piece of gold. We have here taken the Church of England service as our example. Other religious denominations have other rites, though the burial service of the Church is most generally used by all sects; but, however that may be, all the social observances would be the same in every case. Only the family party return to the house. The will is then read in the presence of them all by the family lawyer.

A few years ago it was the custom for all who had attended the funeral to assemble on the following Sunday and appear in church, wearing scarfs and hatbands as on the day of the funeral. Pews were set aside for them, so that they might all be seated in a body. Now there is no ceremony of that kind. The family go, and the officiating clergyman wears a scarf over his surplice if one has been given to him, but no display is made.

Friends and acquaintances express their sympathy after the funeral by leaving or sending their cards, on which they write, underneath their name, "With kind inquiries." When the family feel able to receive callers, they acknowledge these courtesies in a formal manner by sending printed cards, such as this :—

Mrs. WILSON
returns thanks for
Mrs. ABBOTT'S
kind inquiries.

A few words must be said about the monuments placed in the churches, and of the graves themselves in the churchyard or cemetery. Ofttimes the affection of those left behind is at a loss for means wherewith to display its wonted solicitude, and seeks consolation under sorrow in doing honour to all that remains—the silent grave. It is only natural "that filial piety, parental tenderness, and conjugal love should mark with some fond memorial the clay-cold spot where the form, still fostered in the bosom, moulders away." And did affection go no further, who could censure? The wish of Pope, that when he died not a stone might tell where he lay, is a wish that would be granted with extreme reluctance. Though there is a classical simplicity in the turf-clad heap of mould, yet we would fain have something lasting, that will be there, as we say, "for ever," something to keep the spot from the common tread, and the name green in the memory. So be it. Only, let the record be a simple, unaffected one; do not let vanity lead to an excess, sometimes, sad to say, perfectly ludicrous. It may be said that these things are out of date, that the good taste of the nineteenth century forbids and has put down all eulogiums, senseless rhymes, and doggerel on gravestones. Not altogether. Pride, weakness, and vanity still fight for display. Within the last two or three years a monument has been placed in one of the churches of a most learned and ancient city, which records the fact, amongst other details, that the deceased was "the largest single-handed brewer out of London"! A marble monument, however fine the sculpture and costly the material, with an inscription such as this, is far more offensive and outrageous to true taste than the wooden memorial of the ignorant rustic, sculptured with painted bones and decked with death's-heads in all the colours of the rainbow. "It is better that the passer-by, when he sees a name, should recollect the virtues of its owner, than that his remarks should be anticipated by an obtruding narrative."

> "The boast of heraldry, the pomp of pow'r,
> And all that beauty, all that wealth e'er gave,
> Await alike the inevitable hour—
> The paths of glory lead but to the grave."
>
> *Gray.*

INDEX.

A

	PAGE
Affectation, Excessive, to be avoided	39
Amateur Acting	176
Apologising, Excessive, to be avoided	39
Attentions, Gentlemen's, to Ladies	41, 42

B

	PAGE
Balls, Cloak Rooms at	172
——, Decorations at	171
——, Drawing-rooms at	172
——, Duties of Entertainers to Guests at	173
——, Duties of Partners at	174
——, Duties of Stewards at Public	166
——, Fancy Dress	167
——, Introductions at Public	167
——, Lights at	171
——, Management of Public	166
——, Music at	170
——, Private	168
——, Rooms necessary for	168
——, Seasons for	164
——, Tea Rooms at	173
——, Tickets for Public	166
Banns, To be Married by	97
Baptism, Private	28
——, Public	28
Birth, Modern Customs on the occasion of a	27
——, Old Custom on the occasion of a	25
Boating	159
Bowing, Different Modes of	43
Breakfast, Arrangement of the Table for	118
——, Dishes for, at different Seasons	121, 122

218 INDEX.

	PAGE
Breakfast, French	119
——, Hunt and Sportsmen's	120
—— in the Olden Time	116
—— in the Present Day	117
——, Wedding	119
——, What to serve for	118
Bride, Bridegroom's Presents to a	99
——, Costume of a	82, 83
Bridegroom, Gentleman's Dress as a	86
Bridesmaids	95
——, Bridegroom's Presents to the	99
——, Costume of	84

C

Cake and Wine	68
Call, Length of a formal	67
Calling, Use of	62, 63
Calls, Ceremonies of	67, 68
——, Style of Dress when paying	78, 79
——, When they should be paid	63, 64
Cards, How to leave	64
——, Modern	65
——, When to send	65
Carving	136
Ceremony, Extreme, to be avoided	36, 37
Chapel, To be Married at a Licensed	97
Chaperons, Dress of	82
Charades	177
Christening, Ceremony of	30
——, Entertainment given on day of	32
——, Fees for	31
—— Presents	29, 30
——, Style of Dress appropriate for	78
Churching, The rite of	31
Coffee, After Dinner	145
Confirmation	33
——, Age required for	33
——, Ceremony of	33
——, Dress necessary for	33
——, Preparation for	33
Conversation, Remarks on	45, 46

Cookery, Good	133
Courtship, Etiquette of	93, 95
Court, Buckingham Palace	203
——, Gentlemen's Dress at	205
——, Ladies' Dress at	204
——, Who may be presented at	204
—— Mourning	208, 209
——, Irish	208

D

Dancers, Good and bad	169, 170
Dances, Modern fashionable	165
Dancing, Styles of	165
Death, Old Customs on the occurrence of a	211, 212
——, Things to be done immediately on a	210, 211
Dessert, The	144
Dinner à la Russe	136
——, Arrival of Guests to	139
——, Coffee after	145
——, Customs of Wine-taking at	142
——, Departure after a	145
—— en famille	141, 145
——, Going in to	140
——, Retirement of the Ladies from	145
——, Secrets of a Successful	129
—— Table, Appointments and Decorations for	137
——, Tea after	146
——, When to issue Invitations for a	135
——, Whom to invite to	135
—— Question, The	128
——Tables of last Ten Centuries	129—131
Dinners for Different Seasons	146—153
Drawing-room, Rules to be observed at the Queen's	206, 207
Dress, Ball	82
——, Dinner	81
——, Gentlemen's, in former Days	85, 87
——, Gentlemen's, in Modern Times	87
——, Ladies' Morning	81
——, Lawn Tennis	80
——, Neatness in	76

INDEX.

	PAGE
Dress, Suitability in	77
——, Tricycling	200
——, Yachting	80
—— (Court), Gentlemen's	205
——, Ladies'	204

E

Eating and Drinking	114
English, Foreigner's opinion of the	14
Etiquette, Origin of the Word	35

F

Familiarity, Excessive, to be avoided	38
Family, Royal, How to Address the	35
Father-in-law, Interview with the	90
Field Sports	194
Fishing	199
Fun in the Last Century	11
Funerals	210
——, Church Service at	213
——, Dress at	211, 213
——, Expression of Sympathy after	214
——, Sunday after	214

G

Garden Parties, Gentlemen's Dress at	87
——, Ladies' Dress at	79
Gentleman, Characteristics of a	16
——, Definition of a	15
——, Thackeray's Definition of a	17
Gentlemen, Different Classes of the order of	16
Gloves, When to Wear	88
God-parents, Choice of	28, 29

H

Hand, Different Modes of Shaking the	43
Head-dress, a Gentleman's	88
Heraldry	21—23
Honour, Titles of	20, 21
House, Conduct when Staying in a Friend's	72

House, Furniture of a	108—111
Hunting	195—198
——, Gentlemen's Dress for	197
——, Ladies' Dress for	197

I

Inquiries, Acknowledgments for, on a Death	215
Introduction, Laws of	41, 42
——, Letters of	70
Invitations, Forms of	58, 59

J

Jewellery, Gentlemen's	88
——, Ladies'	81

K

Kissing, Foreigners' Remarks on English	72

L

Lady, Definition of a	18, 19
Language, Ruskin's Remarks on	47
Laughter	48
Lawn Tennis	59, 80
Letter, Addison's Opinion on the Style of a	54
——, German Injunction on Writing a	54
——, How to Write a	54
Letters, How to Write, to Strangers	56
——, Proper Terminations to	57
Levée, Ceremony at the	207
Licence, Special	96
——, Ordinary	97
Luncheon, Definition of	123
——, Cold	124
——, Hot	125
——, Manners at	124
——, What to place on the Table for	124, 125

M

	PAGE
Manager, A Good	107, 108
Manners, Dr. Johnson's	40
——, Former French	12
—— in Early Times	9, 10
——, Mark of Good	36
——, Necessity of Good	12, 13
—— of Last Century	10, 11
——, Polished	14
Married, Different Ways to Get	96
Monuments	215, 216
Mourners	213
Mourning	84
——, How Long to Wear	85

N

Neatness in Dress	76
Nobility, How to Address the	38

P

Paper and Envelopes, Different Kinds of	55
Parties, Garden	185
——, Lawn Tennis	186
——, Dresses for Garden	187
Party, Table Requisites for Entertaining a	113, 114
Picnics, Conveyance of Guests and Provisions to	190, 191
——, Election of Managers for	191
——, Private	190
——, Provisions and Beverages at	193
——, Style of Dress for	80
——, Subscription	191
——, Things not to be Forgotten for	192
——, Why People Enjoy	189
Politeness, Lord Chesterfield's Definition of	13
Precedency, Laws of	49
Presents, Christening	29
——, Wedding	93

Q

Queen, Ceremony of Presentation to the	206

R

	PAGE
Rank, Modes of Addressing Letters to Persons of	60, 61
Registrar, Marriage at the Office of a	98
Ring, Engagement	92
——, Wedding	98
Rooms, Breakfast	108
——, Different Styles of	108—111
——, Dining	109
——, Drawing	109, 110
——, Protest against "Best"	111
——, Temperature of	111

S

Seaside, Style of Dress for the	87
Sealing-wax	56
Servants, Gratuities to	73
Shooting, Gentlemen's Dress for	198
——, Organisation of Parties for	198
Skating	201
Speech, Inaccuracies of	48, 49
Supper, Arrangement of Table for	160
——, Ball	164—175
——, French Display at	160, 161
——, Hot	160—162
——, Impromptu	162
——, Roman Bill of Fare for	160

T

Table, Laying the	112
Tables, Our Supper	161
Tableaux Vivants	180
——, Subjects for	180
Teas, High	154
——, Afternoon	154
——, What to put on the Table for	155, 156
Theatricals, Private	176—184
Toast, How to Prepare Sugared	26
Tricycling	200
——, Gentlemen's Dress for	201
——, Ladies' Dress for	200

V

Visiting	62, 74

Visits, Lengths of...	66, 67, 70
Voice, Cultivation of the...	47

W

Waiters	133
Walk, Different Styles of	44, 45
——, Difference between a Man's and a Woman's	45
Wedding Breakfast	103, 121
——, Church Ceremony at a	102
——, Day before the	99
——, Day of the ...	101—103
——, Departure after a ...	104
——, Dress of Guests at a	82—84
——, Guests to be Invited to a ...	99
——, Things to be Thought of previous to a	89, 90
Will, Reading the	214
Wines, Dinner	143
——, After Dinner	144

CPSIA information can be obtained
at www.ICGtesting.com
Printed in the USA
BVHW041509200621
609992BV00001B/87

9 780469 504844